WHAT PEOPLE ARE SAYING:

"YES! YES! YES!!!! The enemy would love nothing more than that a precious servant of the Lord be silenced. What joy that the light has broken through!"

— DEANNE N.

"You are such a wonderful tool for our Lord! Thank you for encouraging me!!"

— ANDREA C.

"I'm daring to ask God for the impossible. Your writings have reignited my faith to believe again. I'm excited!"

— JILL F.

"Your words continue to bless those of us who are going through losses and pain. We can praise Him in the midst of it if we press on. I thank God for the gift of words that He has given you to share with others. Thank you for listening to Him."

— KAREN B.

40 PRAYERS FOR PERILOUS TIMES

POWERFUL INTERCESSORY PRAYERS FOR AN UPSIDE-DOWN WORLD

KELLY LANGSTON

Olde Providence Press

COPYRIGHT

40 PRAYERS FOR PERILOUS TIMES

POWERFUL INTERCESSORY PRAYERS FOR AN UPSIDE-DOWN WORLD

KELLY LANGSTON

Olde Providence Press

COPYRIGHT

To the Secret Army

I lift up my eyes to the mountains—where does my help come from? My help comes from the Lord, the Maker of heaven and earth..

— PSALM 121 (NIV)

CONTENTS

PREFACE

In the summer of 2016, America was on fire.

In the searing heat of the all-too long season, America was in the middle of one of the most divisive elections in the history of our country. Emotions were tender and painfully public, throbbing like an exposed nerve in the salty air of that oppressive summer.

Rage was everywhere, in the constant stream of news reports citing riots, corruption, back-fighting, allegations and embarrassing innuendos, all leading to a feeling of despair and hopelessness.

Worse, political differences violently separated many Americans who were once close personally, tearing apart families, friendships, business cultures and even church communities. It was like an invisible entity was pouring gasoline on a fire that was burning out of control.

America was in trouble.

I recall standing in front of my television screen amazed at what I was seeing. Every night, the reports seem to flame the rage, supplying ample fuel for the fires of discord. Watching those reports night after night, I admit to wondering if America was forever lost. Had we become our own worst enemy? How had we grown to be so prone to bitterness and hatred?

In near despair, I believed that there wasn't much that I could do to help. After all, I was but one small voice, a middle-aged mother and wife trying to make ends meet, and certainly over-looked by most. Who was I to have any kind of impact for a change?

The situation seemed truly hopeless—*or was it?*

Yet, there was one thing that I could do, and maybe—just maybe—that one thing was *exactly why God had chosen to place me here*, in this time and season.

If America needs supernatural help—and believe me, she does—then I want to pray for that heavenly help to come. That kind of massive assistance can only come from one place: from God the Father, and from Jesus the Son, and the Holy Spirit.

I began to pray. At first, my prayers were quiet and hesitant, as if I wondered if God would answer them at all. As time went by, however, I began to add scriptural promises to my prayers, knowing that He is faithful to each one, and believing that God's word will not return void:

FOR AS THE RAIN AND SNOW COME DOWN FROM HEAVEN, AND DO NOT RETURN THERE WITHOUT WATERING THE EARTH, MAKING IT BEAR AND SPROUT, AND PROVIDING SEED TO THE SOWER AND BREAD TO THE EATER, SO WILL MY WORD BE WHICH GOES OUT OF MY MOUTH; IT WILL NOT RETURN TO ME VOID (USELESS, WITHOUT RESULT), WITHOUT ACCOMPLISHING WHAT I DESIRE, AND WITHOUT SUCCEEDING IN THE MATTER FOR WHICH I SENT IT.

— ISAIAH 55:10-11 (AMP)

I scoured the Bible to uncover these precious promises to include them in my prayers, reminding God daily of His Word.

Soon, as you will see as you read, my quiet prayers grew in boldness and audacity, as I began to understand that our right to "approach the throne with boldness" came only by the great and costly sacrifice of Jesus:

THEREFORE LET US [WITH PRIVILEGE] APPROACH THE THRONE OF GRACE [THAT IS, THE THRONE OF GOD'S GRACIOUS FAVOR] WITH CONFIDENCE AND WITHOUT FEAR, SO THAT WE MAY RECEIVE MERCY [FOR OUR FAILURES] AND FIND [HIS AMAZING] GRACE TO HELP IN TIME OF NEED [AN APPROPRIATE BLESSING, COMING JUST AT THE RIGHT MOMENT].

— HEBREWS 4:16 (AMP)

TWO TRUTHS THAT HAVE FOREVER CHANGED ME

First, I know that Christ *died to give us the privilege to approach the Holy throne of God*; and secondly, I know that God honors *every promise* in His word. *Every. Single Promise.*

Amazingly, because of our relationship with Christ, Christians are heirs to these precious promises, including those given to God's chosen people, Israel:

FOR NO MATTER HOW MANY PROMISES GOD HAS MADE, THEY ARE "YES" IN CHRIST. AND SO THROUGH HIM THE "AMEN" IS SPOKEN BY US TO THE GLORY OF GOD.

— 2 CORINTHIANS 1:20 (AMP)

In the dawning of this revelation—a revelation that I am forever grateful to the Holy Spirit for leading me to it—*40 Prayers for Perilous Times* was birthed.

As you read these prayers, know that my prayer for you is that you will realize that we do have a thrilling role to play in God's will for the world in which we live. We are called to be a part of the story—*in prayer*.

Right now, God is seeking people who will humble themselves and pray, who will trust His Word and intercede for our families, for our neighborhoods, and for the nations of this world.

Yes, there exists a *secret army of prayer warriors*, living in simple homes and quiet spaces. The world does not recognize them, but know this: *God does*. He hears their prayers as they remind Him of His Word. As they pray God's Word, angels hearken to it to do His bidding.

Our enemy wants us to believe that our circumstances are hopeless. Because he hates God and all that God loves—including His children—he tells us that we are insignificant and over-powered.

Above all, our enemy does not want us to understand the power of prayer to change our hearts so we will return to the Lord, because if we do, God will honor His promise and heal our land:

IF MY PEOPLE, WHICH ARE CALLED BY MY NAME, SHALL HUMBLE THEMSELVES, AND PRAY, AND SEEK MY FACE, AND TURN FROM THEIR WICKED WAYS; THEN WILL I HEAR FROM HEAVEN, AND WILL FORGIVE THEIR SIN, AND WILL HEAL THEIR LAND.

— 2 CHRONICLES 7:14 (HCSB)

THE CHOICE IS UP TO YOU.

Will you jump in with me in for the next 40 days to pray in one of the most powerful ways we can pray? Will you join me in praying God's Word—reminding Him of His promises to us—in a cry for help?

I hope so, because God is waiting to answer.

INTRODUCTION

HOW TO USE THIS BOOK

Quiet prayers from simple homes will impact the world in ways we cannot begin to imagine.

What if you had special access to God and could approach His heavenly throne at any time?

Would you dare approach The Ancient of Days? The Almighty Creator? And if you did, what would you ask Him?

What if praying could make a tangible difference in today's world? Would you pray more if you knew—beyond a shadow of a doubt—that God would hear and answer? Would you pray if you knew that prayer would impact your neighborhood, your city, and your nation in an astounding way?

The fact is, prayer *can and will* impact the world, and if we study history and the Bible, we can discover evidence of its impact throughout the centuries. Through prayer, we invite God into our story, and when that happens we will see a dramatic change in the world around us.

I'm writing about the kind of prayer that makes mountains move, rocks shake, walls fall, and doors open. You won't see those things happen with wishful thinking or "positive thoughts."

Yes, this is exactly the kind of prayer that God is waiting to hear! If you have this book in hand, it's no accident. He is calling you by name, and He is waiting for you to cry out to Him.

Child of God, you were never meant to be a powerless, ineffective Christian tossed about in the chaotic storms that we see in the news stories today (although our enemy wants us to believe that we are). In truth, God is all-powerful and longing to hear His children cry out to Him for mercy and divine help in a time of need... a perilous time! He's waiting for you to jump into the game!

Will you?

I am convinced that God is calling for an army of warriors who will jump into the battle and fight God's way: in thanksgiving and in prayer.

You are about to discover one of the most overlooked concepts of prayer:

One of the most powerful ways to pray is to remind God, in prayer, of the promises found in His Word.

In this book, you will do just that! For the next 40 days, join me in offering prayers that are *specifically based* on Biblical promises. Because God is unfailingly faithful to His Word, you can be confident that He will answer, because He honors every promise. Every one!

The next 40 days will change your life and impact the world around you. You'll experience the power of praying God's word—by actually doing it!

And there's more: After each of the written prayers, there is a page for you to write your own prayer, followed by a space to record God's responses. Trust me, He will respond! When you begin to include God's promises in your prayers, you will see firsthand the difference of praying in this way.

The right to approach God's throne was purchased and at an extremely costly price.

It was purchased by Jesus, the Son of God, *who died* to give us this right. When we receive Jesus as our Lord and Savior, we have the right to approach the Ancient of Days, because we are approaching the throne *in Christ.* Jesus sits at the right hand of God advocating for us when we do.

So, knowing the price that Jesus paid to give us this right, isn't it time to begin? Are you ready to take that divine gift and use it? I promise you that when you do, it will change your prayer life forever. Prayer will become one of the most thrilling things you can do.

What are you waiting for? Let's begin!

THEREFORE LET US APPROACH THE THRONE OF GRACE WITH BOLDNESS, SO THAT WE MAY RECEIVE MERCY AND FIND GRACE TO HELP US AT THE PROPER TIME.

— HEBREWS 4:16 (HCSB)

DAY 1: CRY OUT TO YAHWEH

And I will do whatever you ask in my name, so that the Father may be glorified in the Son. You may ask me for anything in my name, and I will do it.

— JOHN 14:13-14 (NIV)

*L*ord, I come before You in simplicity today. I bring only myself. I am not dressed up or lofty, just simply "me," drawing near to You—*the Almighty God*—in a perilous time.

I thank you, Lord, for granting me this precious moment to be with You. Thank You for Your provisions today: for food, for shelter and for hearing my prayer. I know that nothing escapes You and that even now, You are aware of everything going on in the world. Despite great despair and pain, You are watching, leaning in, and listening for the cries of Your children.

TODAY, LORD, I AM CRYING OUT TO YOU.

Lord, I see the suffering of so many. I sense their pain, and I see the chaos around me. Each day, it intensifies. When will it end, Lord?

I see so many deceptions, countless lies, and unspeakable evil. I see so many who are struggling to see *Your Light*, while others do all that they can to hide it from them. And yet, I know that they will fail.

DARKNESS WILL ALWAYS GIVE WAY TO LIGHT, AND
YOUR LIGHT HAS ALREADY OVERCOME THIS WORLD.

Today, Lord—in this moment—I draw near to You and ask that You guide me in my steps today.

Open my eyes to the needs around me, and provide for my family today so that we may, in turn, provide for others in need.

Cause me to walk in stillness today so that I may hear Your voice throughout the day.

Help me bring Your Light to someone today who needs encouragement. Help me to be Your eyes, Your arms, Your feet and Your voice so that others may be comforted and know Your Love... the only hope for this world.

I thank You that you offer it to us—this incredible gift of Love —an offering poured out through Jesus' great sacrifice to anyone who will accept it. I thank you, too, that you loved us enough to give us freewill to choose it for ourselves; it is never forced upon us.

I CHOOSE TODAY TO ACCEPT YOUR LOVE. MAY IT SO SHINE IN MY
LIFE THAT OTHERS WILL BE DRAWN TO YOU, TOO.

I ask these things in the precious and Most Holy Name of Jesus. Amen!

Your Prayer: Date:

Prayer answered:

DAY 2: WHAT MUST I DO TO BE HEARD BY YOU?

If I close the sky so there is no rain, or if I command the grasshopper to consume the land, or if I send pestilence on My people, and My people who are called by My name humble themselves, pray and seek My face, and turn from their evil ways, then I will hear from heaven, forgive their sin, and heal their land. My eyes will now be open and My ears attentive to prayer from this place.

— 2 CHRONICLES 7:13-15 (HCSB)

My Father—my God—my ears strain to hear You speak!

I have surrendered my life to Jesus, "the way, the truth and the life." He took my sins and washed them clean in His sacrifice.

I thank you for Jesus, for providing the way to the Father. I am now one of those called by Your Name! I can now approach your throne in safety, covered completely by mercy and grace.

So now, Lord, I boldly come before You in prayer, my Holy Father. I lift my voice to You as a child of God.

I bring all of my concerns to You and lay them now at Your feet. Take them from me, Father, for they are too heavy for me to carry… and I am tired.

Lord, forgive me for turning away from You in so many things. Forgive me for wandering off on my own. I have tried to do things my own way and in my own power, but my efforts have been all in vain.

I am turning back to You now, Father.
You are my hope and victory!

Lord, I cry out to You, asking You to restore our land. Comfort the many people who are hurting today.

Where there are *division and chaos*, bring *Your peace and unity in Christ*. Restore peace once again to the nation, and let it start with my own home. May it be a place of refuge for weary travelers, for those You are calling.

May this neighborhood be a light to our city, and our city a light to our nation. Once again, let our nation be a light to a world in need.

Fill the land with Your Mighty Presence, Lord! Fill it with your Light. Remember your people, and turn our hearts back to you. Let it start with me.

Thank you, Father, for listening to me. Thank You for hearing my prayer. To You be the glory forever!

I ask these things in the name of Jesus, Amen!

Your Prayer: Date:

Prayer answered:

DAY 3: STRENGTH IN THE MIDST OF THE STORM

I pray that He may grant you, according to the riches of His glory, to be strengthened with power in the inner man through His Spirit, and that the Messiah may dwell in your hearts through faith. I pray that you, being rooted and firmly established in love, may be able to comprehend with all the saints what is the length and width, height and depth of God's love, 1and to know the Messiah's love that surpasses knowledge, so you may be filled with all the fullness of God.

— EPHESIANS 3:16-19 (HCSB)

A tree without strong roots will topple in the winds of a raging storm.

What a gift we have in the Holy Spirit, Lord! A gift purchased at such a sacrificial cost. Who am I that such a priceless gift be given?

I am so thankful that through this Spirit, I can be with You, Lord. *I am never alone!*

Vast are the riches of Your wisdom and glory. Oh, Lord, may

Your wisdom guide me today.

TEACH ME YOUR WAYS, LORD, THAT I MAY BE VICTORIOUS IN THE
PLANS THAT YOU HAVE SET BEFORE ME. BEYOND MY WILDEST
IMAGINATION, YOU EMPOWER ME WITH STRENGTH. IN YOU, LORD, I
AM RICH INDEED.

For whatever need I have, and in whatever trial I face today—
both great and small—You promise to provide for me through the
abundance of Your glorious riches. They are never depleted!

Make your home, Lord Jesus, in my heart today. Help me to
trust You fully. When I am pressed, help me to say, "I will trust in
the Lord."

LORD, THE STORM CLOUDS DARKEN THE HORIZON, YET I AM
CONFIDENT THAT YOU HAVE CONQUERED THE STORM. I FEEL THE
MENACING WINDS ON MY CHEEKS, AND I SEE THE DUST CLOUDS
SWIRL AT MY FEET.

But You, Lord, have loved me well. I will stand rooted in Your
extravagant love.

In Your love, Lord may I continue to stand, and through this
great storm may I be a blessing to others.

May I provide shelter to someone in need today.

May I grow spiritually taller in this Love—through Christ—so
that my branches can be a shelter to others who suffer in
the storm.

MAY MY FACE BE EVER LOOKING UPWARD, GLISTENING WITH YOUR
SWEET RADIANCE WHEN THE RAINS HIT.

In this, Lord, may You be glorified. In this, Lord, may Your
kingdom come.

I ask these things in the name of Jesus, Amen!

Your Prayer: Date:

Prayer answered:

Your Prayer: Date:

Prayer answered:

DAY 4: WHERE ARE YOU IN SUFFERING AND PAIN?

I pray that you, being rooted and established in love, may have power, together with all the Lord's holy people, to grasp how wide and long and high and deep is the love of Christ, and to know this love that surpasses knowledge—that you may be filled to the measure of all the fullness of God.

— EPHESIANS 3:17-19 (HCSB)

Father, we are in a mess right now. Everywhere I look, I see sorrow and rage. The earth is moaning in distress. Fear is nipping at my heel.

I HEAR THE WHISPERS OF THOSE WHO DO NOT KNOW YOU. THEY MURMUR, "WHERE IS YOUR GOD?" I CONFESS, FATHER, THAT SOMETIMES I WONDER IT, TOO. I CAN'T HIDE THESE DOUBTS FROM YOU... YOU KNOW MY INNERMOST THOUGHT.

So I come to you now, bringing my questions to You in prayer.

When I don't understand, I go to Your Word. You have the answers that I seek.

Your ways, it says, are not my ways. Your thoughts, Scripture tells me, are higher, so I surrender to Your will. I place every fear at your throne.

Lift me up, Father, in your strong arms so I can see from Your perspective.

How vast is the measure of your love! How wide and long and high and deep! Of it, there is no end!

Everywhere that I go, Father, You are there! I cannot be hidden from You.

Though the enemy tries to discourage me, I am confident that Your plan is unfolding as You have predicted. Every detail is being arranged with perfect precision. In the end, what a beautiful story it will be! You've even written the last chapter, giving it to us as a hope and encouragement.

As I think about this Great Love, there is no place for fear. When I consider it, I am strong.

Your goodness and mercy will surround me all of the days of my life.

And so I choose to trust You, Father. I trust your plan for this world and trust in Your plan for me.

I trust You to be faithful to every promise! Thank you for these precious promises, Father, they are our inheritance.

And thank You for Your Great Love.

I ask these things in the name of Jesus, Amen!

Your Prayer: Date:

_____

_____

_____

_____

_____

_____

_____

_____

_____

_____

_____

_____

_____

_____

_____

_____

_____

Prayer answered:

_____

_____

_____

DAY 5: WHO CAN KNOW THE MIND OF THE LORD?

Oh, the depth of the riches both of the wisdom and the knowledge of God!
How unsearchable His judgments and untraceable His ways! For who
has known the mind of the Lord? Or who has been His counselor?

— ROMANS 11:33-34 (HCSB)

*H*ow astonishingly beautiful are the secrets of the Lord!
How intricate are the details Your plan!

Who am I to understand it? Who dares to question Your ways?

You make a vibrant garden from the dust of the earth. You fashion a rainbow and place it in the clouds after a raging storm.

YOU TAKE WHAT IS MEANT FOR EVIL AND MAKE IT FOR GOOD.

You cause our weakness to be our strength. You create stunning beauty from fragile ashes.

Your grace is limitless; it reaches to the ends of the earth! To every man, woman, and child! Your offer of mercy extends to our broken places where we are confused and deceived.

WHO AM I TO JUDGE WHEN ONLY YOU KNOW THE HIDDEN PLACES OF THE HEART?

Teach me, Lord, to have peace in the "not knowing."
Sing over me and quiet my questions with Your spiritual song.
Remind me that I am not god. No! I was created to walk in your Light and bring You glory.
I was created to enjoy the presence of my God. Think of that!

YOU ARE AT WORK, SECRETLY, BEHIND THE HEADLINES AND THE CLOSED DOORS. WHEN ALL SEEMS LOST AND IN YOUR PERFECT TIMING, WE'LL SEE THE BIG REVEAL! JESUS!

Every knee will bow and tongue confess that Name... when our suffering will be like waters gone by.
Until that day, Lord, I ask these things in the name of Jesus, Amen!

Your Prayer: Date:

_____

_____

_____

_____

_____

_____

_____

_____

_____

_____

_____

_____

_____

_____

_____

_____

_____

Prayer answered: _____

_____

_____

_____

DAY 6: PRAY AS A CHILD OF GOD

Now if we are children, then we are heirs—heirs of God and co-heirs with Christ, if indeed we share in his sufferings in order that we may also share in his glory.

— ROMANS 8:17 (NIV)

*I*n this life, Lord, You've given us choices. *Big choices... small choices.*

Some choices make little difference in our lives, like choosing what to wear on any given day. Others are significant, like choosing a line of work.

Lord, in this country—America—You have blessed us with innumerable, precious choices.

And yet, Lord, we've taken these freedoms for granted.

I'm so sorry, Lord, that I sometimes forget the immeasurable value of the freedom to worship You openly. What an amazing gift it is! Thank You for it, and thank you every drop of blood sacrificed so that we may be counted as a free people.

Still, Lord, there's another gift that is even greater:

THE MYSTERIOUS GIFT OF FREEWILL.

In that gift—*a freedom*—You've given us an extraordinary choice: We have the freedom—through the sacrifice of Christ—to choose to become one of Your own: a child of the Most High God! Or, we can choose to be our own god.

The choice is ours.

How astounding that You've laid this choice at our feet! Every man, woman, and child have been blessed with freewill.

NO RULER CAN SEIZE ANOTHER MAN'S INNERMOST HEART. YOU'VE MADE IT OURS TO GIVE FREELY. THINK ABOUT THAT!

Of all of the choices in life, this is the one that matters most! One choice leads to life everlasting, and the other leads to death.

Lord, I make this choice today—I believe Jesus is God's son, and that He died to save me:

If you confess with your mouth, "Jesus is Lord," and believe in your heart that God raised Him from the dead, you will be saved.

— ROMANS 10:9 (HCSB)

I also believe that Jesus, through His sacrifice on the cross, has completely washed every sin clean, and that through Him, I have full access to the Father as a child of God.

Let us then approach God's throne of grace with confidence, so that we may receive mercy and find grace to help us in our time of need.

— HEBREWS 14:6 (NIV)

So I will lean into You, Jesus, that I may know You and be filled to the measure of Your fullness.

In a perilous time, I need the fullness of You now more than ever!

WE ARE AT WAR, BUT IT'S NOT A WAR AGAINST FLESH AND BLOOD. ONLY AS A CHILD OF GOD CAN WE STAND FIRM IN THIS WAR.

For this reason, I ask You for the measure of all of the fullness of God, as your Word offers me.

Then I can pray in Your Name, in Your authority, and with great expectation!

Your Kingdom Come! Your will be done! To You be glory forever!

I ask these things in the name of Jesus, Amen!

Your Prayer: Date:

Prayer answered:

DAY 7: IT'S TIME TO ASK

I pray that you, being rooted and firmly established in love, may be able to comprehend with all the saints what is the length and width, height and depth of God's love, and to know the Messiah's love that surpasses knowledge, so you may be filled with all the fullness of God.

— EPHESIANS 3:17-21 (HCSB)

Sometimes I'm afraid to ask, Lord. I'm afraid You won't hear me.

I'M AFRAID MY REQUEST ISN'T IMPORTANT.
I'M AFRAID THAT MAYBE YOU DON'T HAVE TIME FOR ME.
OR MAYBE I'M AFRAID THAT YOUR ANSWER WILL BE "NO."

So I haven't asked. But that needs to change because this world is in need, Lord… a terrible need. This isn't the time to be afraid.
SO I'M GOING TO ASK.
See, there's fighting everywhere, Lord. Between nations and

between races. Between friends and families. So much hate. Even murderous hate.

So I've got to ask.

I can't see the reason for so much turmoil, but it's everywhere I look!

We see our neighbors as our enemy, and that's a lie. We see ourselves as worthless, and that's a bigger lie.

We see you as distant, and that's the biggest lie yet.

I know that You're here, waiting. Waiting for Your children to ask. So I'm asking, Lord.

Would you rain down some peace?

Would you send it down to our smoldering souls? Wash away the discontent? The arrogance of our pride?

Would You hold a mirror to our faces so we can see how we look from heaven with our pitchforks raised and our teeth clenched?

Would you rain down some peace today?

Your Word says:

What is the source of wars and fights among you? Don't they come from the cravings that are at war within you? You desire and do not have. You murder and covet and cannot obtain. You fight and war.

— JAMES 4:1-2 (HCSB)

Shine a light on our souls so we can truly see what You want to fix! Open our hard hearts to Your Love again!

Would you rain down some peace, Lord? Some Jesus peace?

Ah, Lord, we are dry. I am dry.

Your Word says:

YOU DO NOT HAVE BECAUSE YOU DO NOT ASK.

— JAMES 4:2 (HCSB)

So I'm asking now. Your Word says:

YOU ASK AND DON'T RECEIVE BECAUSE YOU ASK WITH WRONG MOTIVES, SO THAT YOU MAY SPEND IT ON YOUR EVIL DESIRES.

— JAMES 4:3 (HCSB)

Would You teach me Your will So I can ask the things of Your heart? Things like patience and kindness and humility?

WOULD YOU TEACH ME YOUR TRUTH?
WOULD YOU TEACH ME TO HOPE AGAIN?

I'm asking, Lord, and I know You are here. I know You are leaning down to listen to my prayer.

I'm asking for some Jesus peace.

I'm asking for our nation, and I'm asking for our world.

And would you rain it down, Lord? Rain it down on me.

I ask in the name of Jesus, Amen!

Your Prayer: Date:

_____

Prayer answered:

DAY 8: BE STRONG AND COURAGEOUS

HAVEN'T I COMMANDED YOU: BE STRONG AND COURAGEOUS? DO NOT BE AFRAID OR DISCOURAGED, FOR THE LORD YOUR GOD IS WITH YOU WHEREVER YOU GO."

— JOSHUA 1:9 (HCSB)

I remember, Lord:

Moses was dead and You encouraged Joshua to lead the Israelites into the Promised Land. After 40 years of wandering, it was time for the Israelites to cross the Jordan River.

The land was theirs—but they would have to take possession of it. It wouldn't be easy.

"Be strong and courageous."

He must have been on edge, Joshua, standing in the long shadow of a such a reputable predecessor as Moses.

When the scouts, four decades ago, saw giants in the land, the Israelites quickly lost their faith, though they knew Your will and they knew Your promise, Lord—the promise You whispered to their ancestors *who believed without seeing*. And they had You, Lord, with them.

The Israelites had a choice to make: Believe Your Word and trust in Your promise—or back away in doubt.

Yet, the giants were intimidating and they were afraid, so they choose to live in their circumstances rather than cross into Your promise. With the promise just over the horizon, they turned back.

Forty years passed and Joshua faced the giants once again.

"Be strong and courageous."

It wasn't a suggestion, but a commandment. Joshua chose to believe. He believed in the promise, and he believed that You were with him.

Joshua took possession of the land. It wasn't easy.

TODAY, LORD, I NEED TO TRUST YOU MORE THAN EVER BEFORE— BECAUSE THERE ARE GIANTS IN OUR LAND, TOO. AND I HAVE A CHOICE TO MAKE.

If *"Faith is the assurance of things hoped for, the conviction of things not seen,"* why, then, is it so much easier to believe in the things I see rather than trust Your promises?

I WANT TO SEE, AND I WANT TO TOUCH. YET YOU REQUIRE FAITH.

So do I trust You, even when the situation looks impossible?

I can hear Your words—the words You whispered to Joshua centuries ago as You encouraged him to take the land.

"Be strong and courageous."

Yes, I have a choice, Lord. To trust you—or to turn back.

Give me the strength to make the correct choice! Shield my eyes from the giants that surround me. Lift my head so that I may only see You!

Do not turn from it to the right or to the left, that you may be successful wherever you go.

— JOSHUA 1:7 (NIV)

Lead me, Lord, to walk a straight path, the one you have prepared for me. Keep me from temptation, and deliver me from every evil.

"Be strong and courageous."

Lord, help me not lose heart... even when I see giants in the land.

"Do not be afraid; do not be discouraged."

Let Your joy, Lord, be my strength. Help me to know Your perfect love all the more in times of chaos and trouble.

In Your Love, there is no fear.

For the Lord your God will be with you wherever you go.

— JOSHUA 1:9 (NIV)

I want to reach Your "Promised Land" for my life! I want to go in and take possession of it!

Be with me, Lord, and lead me to the place You have prepared for me. *Drive out the giants in the land!*

Thank you for the rich inheritance of promises, Lord, that you extend to me through Christ Jesus. And always, Lord, to bring You glory. Your faithfulness abounds.

In the name of Jesus, Amen!

Your Prayer: Date:

Prayer answered:

DAY 9: A SERIOUS PRAYER FOR PERILOUS TIMES

EVEN NOW—THIS IS THE LORD'S DECLARATION—TURN TO ME WITH ALL YOUR HEART, WITH FASTING, WEEPING, AND MOURNING.

— JOEL 2:12 (HCSB)

Return to me with all of your heart...
Show me what that means, Lord, for only You know the deepest places of my heart. Break down the walls I've built to keep You at a distance.

Return to me with fasting...

Show me the things that I have idolized, Lord. I lay them at Your feet, every idol that has captured my fickle attentions and kept me from You. Restore my priorities, Lord. I'm placing You first again.

Return to me with weeping.

How many tears have been shed, Lord? How many on this day alone? We have raised our fists to the heavens in defiance. How many times have we pushed you away? Out of our schools, our homes, and our hearts?

Forgive us for turning our backs on You.

We've mocked. We've been self-centered. We've placed so many things before You, Lord, when You offer us so much!

LOVE. SAFETY. AND PRECIOUS FREEDOMS.

Return to me with mourning.

I mourn the days lost when I have wandered so far from Your path. I mourn the choices I have made that caused someone pain. I mourn that I have kept Your Word to myself because I was too afraid to share it.

Forgive me, Lord.

I mourn for our nation when we've allowed our history of faith to be wiped away like chalk on a blackboard. What have we done? How many lies have we allowed ourselves believe?

Forgive us, Lord.

I'm returning to You, asking, will You relent? Will You leave a blessing instead?

RETURN TO THE LORD YOUR GOD, FOR HE IS GRACIOUS AND COMPASSIONATE, SLOW TO ANGER AND ABOUNDING IN LOVE, AND HE RELENTS FROM SENDING CALAMITY. WHO KNOWS? HE MAY TURN AND RELENT AND LEAVE BEHIND A BLESSING—GRAIN OFFERINGS AND DRINK OFFERINGS FOR THE LORD YOUR GOD.

— JOEL 2:13-14 (NIV)

I pray in the name of Jesus, Amen!

Your Prayer: Date:

_____

_____

_____

_____

_____

_____

_____

_____

_____

_____

_____

_____

_____

_____

_____

_____

_____

_____

_____

Prayer answered: _____

_____

_____

_____

DAY 10: NO OTHER GODS ... ONLY YOU

I am the Lord your God, who brought you out of Egypt, out of the land of slavery. You shall have no other gods before me.

— EXODUS 20:1-3 (NIV)

I come to You, Lord, in a perilous time. Would you hear my prayers today?

"NO OTHER GODS," YOU SAY.

Other gods? Of course not, Lord! There is only You.

You... and work and play and food everything that fills the minutes and hours of my day.

But no other gods!

Only family and friends and projects and school and ambitions and home and decor.

But no other gods, Lord! Not in my life. And yet...

How many hours of my day are filled with these "gods?"

How many hours do I wander away?

How many times do you wait for me?

You wait while I rise and sip coffee and eat and dress. Wait while the news tickers dance on and on, and until I am late for work again.

You wait, patiently, while I finish the dishes and the laundry and tuck away the kids and all the details of my day.

But I have no other gods! Only You.

And yet….You whisper my name when I rise:

"COME, SPEND SOME TIME WITH ME!"

You walk beside me in the heat of the day:

"LET ME GUIDE YOUR WAY!"

Your presence is with me when the darkness falls:

"COME! I'LL COMFORT YOU WITH SWEET REST! NO OTHER GODS, JUST ME."

I have many requests for our nation, Lord, but first, show me where I've wandered astray. Uncover the idols that keep me from a closer walk with You.

Search me and reveal the things that steal my heart away. Strengthen me to put You first—only You! Clean out the cobwebs of my heart.

No likeness of anything in heaven above... Nothing in the earth beneath, or in the water under the earth...

Yes, Lord, I ask you to turn our hearts back to You, Lord—but let it start with me. Sweet grace flows from heaven above. We are dry in this perilous time!

KNOW THAT THE LORD HAS SET APART THE FAITHFUL FOR HIMSELF; THE LORD WILL HEAR WHEN I CALL TO HIM.

— PSALM 4:3 (HCSB)

In the name of Jesus, Amen!

Your Prayer: Date:

Prayer answered:

DAY 11: FINDING REST IN A PERILOUS TIME

THEREFORE LET ALL THE FAITHFUL PRAY TO YOU WHILE YOU MAY BE FOUND; SURELY THE RISING OF THE MIGHTY WATERS WILL NOT REACH THEM. YOU ARE MY HIDING PLACE; YOU WILL PROTECT ME FROM TROUBLE AND SURROUND ME WITH SONGS OF DELIVERANCE.

— PSALM 32:6-7 (NIV)

I come to you now in stillness.
The world is raging, Lord, but you are calling me to rest.

From morning to night, the noise of the day's chaos is deafening.

So many messages to process, of wars and mayhem and sorrows.

I am so weary of it all.

Yet in the midst of this battle, Lord, you provide me with a place to rest.

A place to close my eyes and breathe deep.

Dark clouds are menacing. The thunder rolls in the distance,
But with you, I have nothing to fear. The battle is already won!

No matter how high the waves roll, Lord, you calm the
rough waters and give me sweet peace.

Sweet Jesus peace.
You could have required so much of me, Lord. You could have
asked me to go on the offensive. To attack and slay the world's
dragons.

Or live up to impossible standards… but that's not you at
all, Lord.

How refreshing to know that it's you who reached down
to me.

This Jesus salvation is a gift that I'll never earn. The price has
been paid.

It's finished. Complete!

You ask only that I receive.

Tonight the world moans and grumbles, but I will lie down
and sleep tonight.

Yes, in stillness and peace, Lord, I'll sleep.

Wars rage on and chaos rumbles through the streets, but you
watch over my sleep and send me peace.

Sweet Jesus peace.

I will praise You, Jesus, Amen!

Your Prayer: Date:

Prayer answered:

DAY 12: THE SECRET IN PRAYING TOGETHER

B Y YOURSELF YOU'RE UNPROTECTED. WITH A FRIEND YOU CAN FACE THE WORST. CAN YOU ROUND UP A THIRD? A THREE-STRANDED ROPE ISN'T EASILY SNAPPED.

— ECCLESIASTES 4:12 (MSG)

Swimming upstream.

That's what it feels like, Lord.

I struggle to keep a forward momentum, a rush of icy water push-back. Sometimes, Lord, I'm not sure if I'm making any progress at all.

My friends say they feel it, too. What was once so easy and clear—is now arduous.

Like swimming upstream in a murky river. The dam has cracked and the waters are rising, *but we aren't home yet.*

The Spirit unites God's children, and I can see it in their eyes. This shifting, this sifting.

It started slowly—almost imperceptibly—but now we can feel it, too. Your people are reaching out to one another. We don't want to journey alone:

FOR WE WERE ALL BAPTIZED BY ONE SPIRIT INTO ONE BODY—WHETHER JEWS OR GREEKS, WHETHER SLAVES OR FREE—AND WE WERE ALL MADE TO DRINK OF ONE SPIRIT.

— 1 CORINTHIANS 12:13 (HCSB)

I walked down the street yesterday and saw a man in the Jesus ball cap. I had never seen him before, but I knew I had to speak to him.

To let him know we had Someone in common.

I think he felt it, too. We laughed like siblings, and it was nice, Lord.

A familiar face in this foreign place, *as we are journeying home.*

You never meant for us to be alone, so help me, Father, to reach out bravely. Open my eyes to those who are your hands and feet to this world in need.

IRON SHARPENS IRON, AND ONE MAN SHARPENS ANOTHER.

— PROVERBS 27:17 (HCSB)

Thank you for these well-timed friendships. I need them right now.

We are stronger together, and it's too costly to let opportunities pass. So lead me to knock on a neighbor's door.

Lord, as it began, let us meet again in homes.

To pray together.
To break bread together.
To encourage one another.

Let us see these tangible evidence of your Great Love.

Tonight, I pray for my friends in Christ. Lift them up tonight, Lord. Watch over them as they sleep.

Give them rest for the day ahead and let them know that, praise God, we are not alone— and we never will be.

I ask these things in the name of Jesus, Amen!

Your Prayer: Date:

_____

_____

_____

_____

_____

_____

_____

_____

_____

_____

_____

_____

_____

_____

_____

_____

_____

Prayer answered:

_____

_____

_____

DAY 13: IN THE WAITING HOURS

I WOULD HAVE DESPAIRED HAD I NOT BELIEVED THAT I WOULD SEE THE GOODNESS OF THE LORD IN THE LAND OF THE LIVING.

— PSALM 27:13 (AMP)

*W*aiting.
Minutes to Hours. Hours to Days.
Days to Weeks. Weeks to Months.
We are waiting, Lord, in these perilous times.
We are waiting for You *to act.*
We are waiting for You *to rise up and defend us.*
We are waiting, Father, for You *to restore our land.*
More than that, Lord, we are waiting for You *to make us whole again.*

The morning's light barely rises over the horizon and already the news reports filter in. They are there whenever I turn on the television. And in the car, when all I want is music to ease my anxious soul. In the coffee shop, too, and at work, or in a line at the grocery store.

The talk is all the same: *politics and greed and hate.*

But You, Lord, You offer something better.

You offer *living hope.*

Not an empty hope, but hope with a promise of fulfillment:

NONE OF THE GOOD PROMISES THE LORD HAD MADE TO THE HOUSE OF ISRAEL FAILED. EVERYTHING WAS FULFILLED.

— JOSHUA 21:45 (HCSB)

And not an empty promise, but a promise from One who is faithful to each one:

BUT THE LORD IS FAITHFUL; HE WILL STRENGTHEN AND GUARD YOU FROM THE EVIL ONE.

— 2 THESSALONIANS 3:3 (HCSB)

You offer goodness in the land of the living.

You offer a hope that can be found:

I WILL BE FOUND BY YOU"—THIS IS THE LORD'S DECLARATION—"AND I WILL RESTORE YOUR FORTUNES AND GATHER YOU FROM ALL THE NATIONS AND PLACES WHERE I BANISHED YOU"—THIS IS THE LORD'S DECLARATION. "I WILL RESTORE YOU TO THE PLACE I DEPORTED YOU FROM."

— JEREMIAH 29:14 (HCSB)

Hope for the future...and hope for right now!

SO IN THE WAITING HOURS...

I WILL NOT LET THE ENEMY SNATCH AWAY MY HOPE.

In the waiting hours...

I WILL REMEMBER YOUR PROMISES,
AND I WILL REMIND YOU OF THEM EVERY DAY!

In the waiting hours...

I WILL SAY, "I TRUST IN YOU, LORD!"
I KNOW YOU HAVE A PLAN FOR ME. I HAVE A FUTURE AND A HOPE.

*LET US HOLD ON TO THE CONFESSION OF OUR HOPE WITHOUT WAVERING,
FOR HE WHO PROMISED IS FAITHFUL.*

— HEBREWS 10:23 (HCSB)

I ask these things in the name of Jesus, Amen!

Your Prayer: Date:

_____

_____

_____

_____

_____

_____

_____

_____

_____

_____

_____

_____

_____

_____

_____

_____

_____

_____

_____

Prayer answered:

_____

_____

_____

DAY 14: DO NOT BE DECEIVED

Be careful that you are not enticed to turn aside, worship, and bow down to other gods. Then the Lord's anger will burn against you. He will close the sky, and there will be no rain; the land will not yield its produce, and you will perish quickly from the good land the Lord is giving you.

— DEUTERONOMY 11:16-17 (HCSB)

If ever there was a need to hear Your voice clearly, Father, it is now.

There are so many conflicting perspectives, and deception is everywhere.

It's a game of smoke and mirrors. A river of twisted words and spun tales.

We could easily drown if it were not for Your protection.

Whom are we to believe?

In these perilous times, Lord, help us know the truth. Deception runs wild, but even so, we don't have to be deceived:

Don't be deceived: God is not mocked. For whatever a man sows he will also reap, because the one who sows to his flesh will reap corruption from the flesh, but the one who sows to the Spirit will reap eternal life from the Spirit.

— GALATIANS 6:7-8 (HCSB)

Because You, Jesus, have sent us the Holy Spirit. He promises to guide us into Your truth:

When the Spirit of truth comes, He will guide you into all the truth. For He will not speak on His own, but He will speak whatever He hears. He will also declare to you what is to come.

— JOHN 16:13 (HCSB)

So lead us, Lord, and keep us from evil.

How easy to be lured away from You—if only briefly.

Just for a moment, they say. Who would find fault in one simple gesture? One misplaced prayer? one nod to another god?

Make no mistake… this is no child's game:

For our battle is not against flesh and blood, but against the rulers, against the authorities, against the world powers of this darkness, against the spiritual forces of evil in the heavens.

— EPHESIANS 6:12 (HCSB)

A small step to the right or the left is all it takes. Before we know it, we're lost:

Above all, be strong and very courageous to carefully observe the whole instruction My servant Moses commanded you. Do

NOT TURN FROM IT TO THE RIGHT OR THE LEFT, SO THAT YOU WILL HAVE
SUCCESS WHEREVER YOU GO.

— JOSHUA 1:7 (HCSB)

Pull us from this river of lies and put our feet on a sure foundation of truth. Disclose the untruths—one by one—even the white lies, too!

Your Word is truth, Lord. Shield our hearts from the enemy's clatter. Speak Your wisdom to our hearts and let us know Your way.

In these times—perilous times—draw us closer to You.

WHEN THE SPIRIT OF TRUTH COMES, HE WILL GUIDE YOU INTO ALL THE
TRUTH. FOR HE WILL NOT SPEAK ON HIS OWN, BUT HE WILL SPEAK
WHATEVER HE HEARS. HE WILL ALSO DECLARE TO YOU WHAT IS TO COME.

— JOHN 16:13 (HCSB)

I ask these things Jesus' name, Amen!

Your Prayer: Date:

Prayer answered:

DAY 15: LAUGHTER IN PERILOUS TIMES

He will yet fill your mouth with laughter and your lips with a shout of joy.

— JOB 8:21 (HCSB)

I want to laugh again, Lord!

Not just a chuckle, but a full-blown, rolling belly laugh. It seems like it's been so long since I had a really good laugh.

I hear you say softly, "Look up."

So I do, noticing the considerable arc my neck makes to turn my gaze from the little screen in the palm of my hand to the bright sky above. Suddenly my two-dimensional world changes to all-out 3-D.

The sky is still the same shade of Carolina blue as it always was, but it seems more vivid somehow. The clouds are piled like mile-high mountains floating over my head.

Lord, that I have been missing this view! I've been missing a carefree life!

It amazes me, Lord, that this is how you call us to live—really live—in Christ.

Without worries, and without fear:

I SOUGHT THE LORD, AND HE ANSWERED ME AND DELIVERED ME FROM ALL MY FEARS.

— PSALM 34:4 (HCSB)

An abundant life—not for the future, but here and now:

A THIEF COMES ONLY TO STEAL AND TO KILL AND TO DESTROY. I HAVE COME SO THAT THEY MAY HAVE LIFE AND HAVE IT IN ABUNDANCE.

— JOHN 10:10 (HCSB)

And to live as free! In Christ, we are truly free!

IF THE SON SETS YOU FREE, YOU WILL BE FREE INDEED.

— JOHN 8:30-36 (NIV)

Why, then, Lord, have I been so discouraged? When did I stop seeing the daily gifts You've given me?

Gifts like the smiles on a stranger's face. Or the flash of a bluebird in my yard. And the sound of children's laughter in the yard.

Loads of rolling laughter.

I've been missing it, Lord.

Thank you, Sweet Father, for this gift of laughter. I'm so glad that You laugh, too.

Amen!

Blessed are you who hunger now, for you will be satisfied.
Blessed are you who weep now, for you will laugh.

— LUKE 6:21 (NIV)

Your Prayer: Date:

_____

_____

_____

_____

_____

_____

_____

_____

_____

_____

_____

_____

_____

_____

_____

_____

_____

_____

Prayer answered:

_____

_____

_____

DAY 16: ALL THINGS

We know that all things work together for the good of those who love God: those who are called according to His purpose.

— ROMANS 8:28 (HCSB)

All things.
    Not some things, or a few things.
Not most things, or some things most of the time.
All things, all of the time.
It's a promise *I remind You of* now with this prayer.
A promise that gives me great comfort. A confidence and peace that cannot be shaken:

FOR THOSE WHO LOVE YOU, LORD, ALL THINGS WORK TO OUR GOOD.

All things.
This is a miracle of Christian living and I see it every day.
You take our sorrows—our ashes—and make something beau-

tiful out of them. You create a tapestry out of the colors of our life:

> To bestow on them a crown of beauty instead of ashes, the oil of joy instead of mourning, and a garment of praise instead of a spirit of despair.
>
> — ISAIAH 61:3 (NIV)

You take my hungry years and use them to strengthen my faith.

> *Scarcity proves that You provide.*
> *Illness demonstrates Your faithfulness to every promise.*
> *And failure brings me to a better place that You've*
> *prepared for me.*
> *Even when I stumble, I fall into Your greater plan!*

Sometimes, Lord, I confess that I forget the promise. I get weighed down in circumstances, focusing too much on the news of the day.

It's like struggling in quicksand, I can't seem to get my footing.

Days when it seems that all is lost and the enemy is winning.

Yet nothing could be further from the truth!

When I'm so beaten me down that I cannot lift a prayer, even then, You meet me where I am.

Your Sweet Spirit lifts prayers on my behalf. All the way to Heaven's throne. Consider that!

I am covered in prayer at all times!

So though night has fallen on the rocky path I walk, I am not afraid, because You are with me.

Your Presence is an unquenchable Light. I can never be lost again!

And one day... one sweet day...

I'll stand astonished when You pull away the curtain—at last!

Then every eye will see that it's been You, Lord, all along, weaving the tiniest of details into perfect place.

We'll wonder together—for a thousand years and more!—at the beauty of Your story. *A glorious, eternal story.*

Let it be as You've declared it to be, Lord Jesus, Amen!

Your Prayer: Date:

_____

_____

_____

_____

_____

_____

_____

_____

_____

_____

_____

_____

_____

_____

_____

_____

_____

_____

Prayer answered:

_____

_____

_____

DAY 17: WHEN SHOULD I SPEAK?

WORDS KILL, WORDS GIVE LIFE; THEY'RE EITHER POISON OR FRUIT—YOU CHOOSE.

— PROVERBS 18:21 (MSG)

There are times to speak out, and times to be silent. Sometimes, Lord, I'm not sure what to do, and it's only getting harder.

Especially in perilous times.

We are called to speak out for those who need Your Love:

THEN HE SAID TO THEM, "GO INTO ALL THE WORLD AND PREACH THE GOSPEL TO THE WHOLE CREATION."

— MARK 16:15 (HCSB)

We are called to share Your Word. To be a Light to a dark world. But honestly, Lord, there's so much push back right now.

And so much offense:

AT THAT TIME MANY WILL BE OFFENDED AND REPELLED [BY THEIR ASSOCIATION WITH ME] AND WILL FALL AWAY [FROM THE ONE WHOM THEY SHOULD TRUST] AND WILL BETRAY ONE ANOTHER [HANDING OVER BELIEVERS TO THEIR PERSECUTORS] AND WILL HATE ONE ANOTHER.

— MATTHEW 24:10 (AMP)

It's so much easier to remain silent. *But I can't.*

See, Lord, the sun set long ago and it's getting darker by the hour.

Dark. Divided. And chaotic.

And there's this: I know that Your Word has the antidote for the darkness. Your Words—are Life:

SIMON PETER ANSWERED, "LORD, WHO WILL WE GO TO? YOU HAVE THE WORDS OF ETERNAL LIFE.

— JOHN 6:68 (HCSB)

I know that You are good... really good:

FOR THE LORD IS GOOD AND HIS LOVE ENDURES FOREVER; HIS FAITHFULNESS CONTINUES THROUGH ALL GENERATIONS.

— PSALM 100:5 (NIV)

I know that You heal our wounds and carry our burdens and lift us out of the muck and mire. So how can I be silent?

And yet... there is a time to be silent.

So this is my prayer tonight, Lord: Would You help me know the difference? Would You give me the wisdom to know when I should speak up... and when I should not?

Would You help me listen more, and teach me Your Words and Your ways?

Would You whisper Your Words and bring them to mind?

Lord, help me speak and teach me what to say:

NOW GO! I WILL HELP YOU SPEAK AND I WILL TEACH YOU WHAT TO SAY."

— EXODUS 4:12 (HCSB)

Teach me the discipline to hold my tongue in anger. Never let me speak a hurtful word in anger, nor a word to lead someone astray.

Teach me to speak words of life—encouraging words—never curses:

DEATH AND LIFE ARE IN THE POWER OF THE TONGUE, AND THOSE WHO LOVE IT AND INDULGE IT WILL EAT ITS FRUIT AND BEAR THE CONSEQUENCES OF THEIR WORDS.

— PROVERBS 18:21 (AMP)

Above all, Lord, give me the wisdom, Lord, to know when to speak and when to remain silent.

I ask these things in the name of Jesus, Amen!

THEN THE LORD SAID TO PAUL IN A NIGHT VISION, "DON'T BE AFRAID, BUT KEEP ON SPEAKING AND DON'T BE SILENT. FOR I AM WITH YOU, AND NO ONE WILL LAY A HAND ON YOU TO HURT YOU, BECAUSE I HAVE MANY PEOPLE IN THIS CITY."

— ACTS 18:9-10 (HCSB)

Your Prayer: Date:

Prayer answered:

DAY 18: I KNOW YOU ARE HERE WITH ME

And surely I am with you always, to the very end of the age

— MATTHEW 28:20 (NIV)

It's hard to wrap my mind around this truth, Jesus.
To think that You shared God's glory before the world began, and then gave it up to walk in Jerusalem's dust so that we might know the Father, too.

You've alway been here.

You were the Word that created all things, breathing life into creation:

In the beginning was the Word, and the Word was with God, and the Word was God. He was with God in the beginning. All things were created through Him, and apart from Him not one thing was created that has been created.

— JOHN 1:1-3 (HCSB)

You were God's ram in the thicket—taking our place:

ABRAHAM LOOKED UP AND THERE IN A THICKET HE SAW A RAM CAUGHT BY ITS HORNS. HE WENT OVER AND TOOK THE RAM AND SACRIFICED IT AS A BURNT OFFERING INSTEAD OF HIS SON.

— GENESIS 22:13 (NIV)

You were the fragile baby in a manger—Immanuel, God with us!

SEE, THE VIRGIN WILL BECOME PREGNANT AND GIVE BIRTH TO A SON, AND THEY WILL NAME HIM IMMANUEL, WHICH IS TRANSLATED "GOD IS WITH US."

— MATTHEW 1:23 (HCSB)

You were there, lifted high on the cross and there, lowered to the grave.

You tore the veil—earth-shaking, rocks splitting!—then rose again victorious over death:

AT THAT MOMENT THE CURTAIN OF THE TEMPLE WAS TORN IN TWO FROM TOP TO BOTTOM. THE EARTH SHOOK, THE ROCKS SPLIT AND THE TOMBS BROKE OPEN. THE BODIES OF MANY HOLY PEOPLE WHO HAD DIED WERE RAISED TO LIFE.

— MATTHEW 27:51-52 (NIV)

You sit at God's right hand!

FOR THE JOY SET BEFORE HIM HE ENDURED THE CROSS, SCORNING ITS SHAME, AND SAT DOWN AT THE RIGHT HAND OF THE THRONE OF GOD.

— HEBREWS 12:2 (NIV)

And You are with us in perilous times.

You sent the Spirit so we will never be alone in this world. Father. Son. Spirit—Holy Trinity!

BUT I TELL YOU THE TRUTH, IT IS TO YOUR ADVANTAGE THAT I GO AWAY; FOR IF I DO NOT GO AWAY, THE HELPER (COMFORTER, ADVOCATE, INTERCESSOR—COUNSELOR, STRENGTHENER, STANDBY) WILL NOT COME TO YOU; BUT IF I GO, I WILL SEND HIM (THE HOLY SPIRIT) TO YOU [TO BE IN CLOSE FELLOWSHIP WITH YOU].

— JOHN 16:7 (AMP)

You are with me in times of joy and with me in times of uncertainty. Even to the end of the age!

And You are with me now.

So why should I fear or be discouraged? Why should I cower in a corner or walk in sorrow?

No!

I will not fear because I know Your promises are true.

I WILL NOT FEAR THE FUTURE BECAUSE YOU CALLED THIS BATTLE EARLY, AND REST ASSURED... IT'S WON!

So, Lord, when I rise tomorrow, let me walk in complete assurance that wherever I go and whatever comes my way, I face it in not in my power, *but Yours.*

Let my life be a jubilant victory lap home to the place I belong. Why should it not?

Praise You, Jesus, the Overcomer! Amen!

Your Prayer: Date:

Prayer answered:

DAY 19: WINNING THE ULTIMATE RACE

Keep your eyes on Jesus, who both began and finished this race we're in. Study how he did it. Because he never lost sight of where he was headed—that exhilarating finish in and with God—he could put up with anything along the way: Cross, shame, whatever. And now he's there, in the place of honor, right alongside God.

— HEBREWS 12:1-3 (MSG)

In the heat of the race, Lord, I see mirages.
I'm craving water, but when I turn and reach the place where the water glistened just moments before, it's not there. I find only waves of heat and tarry asphalt. What seemed inviting from a distance leaves me empty and dry. The hotter the day, the more mirages I see.

Oh, Lord, I've run races before, but not like this one. *This one is different: it's the ultimate race.* A race to a spiritual prize—an eternal prize. The finish line is there, over the horizon, just beyond the finish line. I can feel it there, deep within my weariness.

My tongue is thick and dry and the watering stations are all but gone, Lord. And there they are, *these mirages*, beckoning me astray.

If I look left or right, I see dancing pools of water enticing me —Come! Drink deep the lies and deceptions. Your thirst will be satisfied.

But I know, Lord—*I know!*— these are only mirages. See, Lord, I've come up empty before.

So I'll keep running.

There is no cheering crowd or music of brass to encourage me onward. No ticker-tape parades or ceremonies of fame.

Only Your quiet words in the deepest part of my soul, saying, "Press on!"

Not that I have already obtained all this, or have already arrived at my goal, but I press on to take hold of that for which Christ Jesus took hold of me. Brothers and sisters, I do not consider myself yet to have taken hold of it. But one thing I do: Forgetting what is behind and straining toward what is ahead, I press on toward the goal to win the prize for which God has called me heavenward in Christ Jesus.

— PHILIPPIANS 3:12-17 (NIV)

No, there's no glory here on this road, at least not in this time. It comes with the words, "Well done."

His master replied, 'Well done, good and faithful servant! You have been faithful with a few things; I will put you in charge of many things. Come and share your master's happiness!'

— MATTHEW 25:21 (NIV)

I am tired, Lord, so be my strength today. Help me take this race step-by-step.

When I stumble, Lord, pick me up again. If I should get lost, show me the way!

When mirages tempt me to turn to the right or left, offering me false promises of anything other than Your will, would You usher me onward?

OH, THE STAKES ARE HIGH, AND I WANT THAT PRIZE! I WANT IT ALL, LORD!

Isn't that what Christ died to give me? A place across that line?

And Lord, if there's a chance that I can help someone else struggling to finish, too.

I'm willing.

I ask these things that You may be glorified in my race, Jesus. Amen!

Your Prayer: Date:

Prayer answered:

DAY 20: WHEN THE BATTLE IS IMMINENT

THEN HE CONSULTED WITH THE PEOPLE AND APPOINTED SOME TO SING FOR THE LORD AND SOME TO PRAISE THE SPLENDOR OF HIS HOLINESS. WHEN THEY WENT OUT IN FRONT OF THE ARMED FORCES, THEY KEPT SINGING:

GIVE THANKS TO THE LORD, FOR HIS FAITHFUL LOVE ENDURES FOREVER.

— 2 CHRONICLES 20:21 (HCSB)

---

*H*ow surprising are Your ways, Lord, *that we should sing in the face of impending battle!*

That's the way Biblical battles were won.

Lord, You choose unusual warriors:

Underdogs. Overlooked. Orphaned and abandoned.

You choose armies that are outnumbered. Armies of one—like David who defeated Goliath while still a boy.

And Gideon's band of 300 men, victorious against a multitude of enemies like locusts, too numerous to be counted!

Now the Midianites, Amalekites, and all the Qedemites had settled down in the valley like a swarm of locusts, and their camels were as innumerable as the sand on the seashore.

— JUDGES 7:12 (HCSB)

So lead us in this battle, Lord! We will march in circles if you desire, like Joshua and the Israelites as they circled Jericho. We'll face towering walls that keep us from Your promise and watch them crumble with a shout.

So the people shouted, and the trumpets sounded. When they heard the blast of the trumpet, the people gave a great shout, and the wall collapsed. The people advanced into the city, each man straight ahead, and they captured the city.

— JOSHUA 6:20 (HCSB)

We will sing Your praises until the trumpet sounds and You descend victorious with a shout!

For the Lord Himself will descend from heaven with a shout, with the archangel's voice, and with the trumpet of God, and the dead in Christ will rise first.

— 1 THESSALONIANS 4:16 (HCSB)

We'll battle from *quiet homes on knees in prayer*!
We'll enter in *with songs of praise*!
We'll fight by *standing firm with hearts on fire for You*!
Lord, confuse our enemies with the sounds of our praise. Defeat them with our song!
Let the world know that You alone are God.
And we shall see that with our shouts, *walls will come down.*

With our songs of praise, *our enemies will be defeated.*
With simple warriors, *giants will be defeated.*

> *Give thanks to the Lord,*
> *for His faithful love endures forever.*

In the name of Jesus, Amen!

Your Prayer: Date:

Prayer answered:

DAY 21: BE STILL

He says, "Be still, and know that I am God; I will be exalted among the nations, I will be exalted in the earth."

— PSALM 46:10: (NIV)

L ord, sometimes I am restless in the waiting.
You whisper, "Just be still."
Sometimes, I struggle for words but find not a one.
You say, "It's okay, the Spirit intercedes for you."

In the same way, the Spirit helps us in our weakness. We do not know what we ought to pray for, but the Spirit himself intercedes for us through wordless groans. And he who searches our hearts knows the mind of the Spirit, because the Spirit intercedes for God's people in accordance with the will of God.

— ROMANS 8:26-27 (NIV)

Sometimes, I long for answers but find countless questions. You pull me close, saying, *"Trust me."*

TRUST IN THE LORD WITH ALL YOUR HEART AND LEAN NOT ON YOUR OWN UNDERSTANDING; IN ALL YOUR WAYS SUBMIT TO HIM, AND HE WILL MAKE YOUR PATHS STRAIGHT.

— PROVERBS 3:5-6 (NIV)

Sometimes, I am discouraged and ready to quit. You prepare a table for me and call me to rest.

YOU PREPARE A TABLE BEFORE ME IN THE PRESENCE OF MY ENEMIES. YOU ANOINT MY HEAD WITH OIL; MY CUP OVERFLOWS.

— PSALM 23 (NIV)

Sometimes I feel forgotten and small. You show me my name written on the palm of Your hand.

LOOK, I HAVE INSCRIBED YOU ON THE PALMS OF MY HANDS; YOUR WALLS ARE CONTINUALLY BEFORE ME.

— ISAIAH 49:16 (HCSB)

Sometimes the future looks bleak and hopeless. You tell me about the New Jerusalem and the river of life that runs through it.

THEN THE ANGEL SHOWED ME THE RIVER OF THE WATER OF LIFE, AS CLEAR AS CRYSTAL, FLOWING FROM THE THRONE OF GOD AND OF THE LAMB DOWN THE MIDDLE OF THE GREAT STREET OF THE CITY. ON EACH SIDE OF THE RIVER STOOD THE TREE OF LIFE, BEARING TWELVE CROPS OF FRUIT, YIELDING ITS FRUIT EVERY MONTH. AND THE LEAVES OF THE TREE ARE FOR THE HEALING OF THE NATIONS. NO LONGER WILL THERE BE ANY

CURSE. THE THRONE OF GOD AND OF THE LAMB WILL BE IN THE CITY, AND HIS SERVANTS WILL SERVE HIM. THEY WILL SEE HIS FACE, AND HIS NAME WILL BE ON THEIR FOREHEADS. THERE WILL BE NO MORE NIGHT. THEY WILL NOT NEED THE LIGHT OF A LAMP OR THE LIGHT OF THE SUN, FOR THE LORD GOD WILL GIVE THEM LIGHT. AND THEY WILL REIGN FOR EVER AND EVER.

— REVELATION 22:1-5 (NIV)

Sometimes people turn me away. You remind me that You have not rejected me.

I TOOK YOU FROM THE ENDS OF THE EARTH, FROM ITS FARTHEST CORNERS I CALLED YOU. I SAID, 'YOU ARE MY SERVANT'; I HAVE CHOSEN YOU AND HAVE NOT REJECTED YOU.

— ISAIAH 41:9 (NIV)

Sometimes, I want to shout and sing. You dance and sing over me while I do.

THE LORD YOUR GOD IS WITH YOU, THE MIGHTY WARRIOR WHO SAVES. HE WILL TAKE GREAT DELIGHT IN YOU; IN HIS LOVE HE WILL NO LONGER REBUKE YOU, BUT WILL REJOICE OVER YOU WITH SINGING."

— ZEPHANIAH 3:17 (NIV)

Sometimes I try too hard. You remind me to laugh.

SARAH SAID, "GOD HAS MADE ME LAUGH; ALL WHO HEAR [ABOUT OUR GOOD NEWS] WILL LAUGH WITH ME."

— GENESIS 21:6 (AMP)

Sometimes I make a colossal mess of my life. You promise new mercies come with the dawn.

BECAUSE OF THE LORD'S FAITHFUL LOVE WE DO NOT PERISH, FOR HIS MERCIES NEVER END. THEY ARE NEW EVERY MORNING; GREAT IS YOUR FAITHFULNESS!

— LAMENTATIONS 3:22-23 (HCSB)

And I wonder....

What have I done to deserve such mercy and grace? Such never-ending love?

You tell me, *"Nothing....nothing at all. Just open Your heart and receive."*

And so... I do. I receive Your great love for me.

Praise to the Father and His Son, Jesus, Amen!

Your Prayer: Date:

Prayer answered:

DAY 22: WATCHING AND WAITING

ELIJAH CLIMBED TO THE TOP OF CARMEL, BENT DOWN TO THE GROUND AND PUT HIS FACE BETWEEN HIS KNEES.

"GO AND LOOK TOWARD THE SEA," HE TOLD HIS SERVANT. AND HE WENT UP AND LOOKED.

"THERE IS NOTHING THERE," HE SAID.

SEVEN TIMES ELIJAH SAID, "GO BACK."

THE SEVENTH TIME THE SERVANT REPORTED, "A CLOUD AS SMALL AS A MAN'S HAND IS RISING FROM THE SEA."

— 1 KINGS 18:42-44 (NIV)

Seven times, Lord.

I think of Elijah, Your prophet, who was called to declare an end to the three-year drought sent because a wicked king and his Baal-loving wife polluted Your people's worship.

Elijah, the prophet, who insisted that Your people make a decision: Choose once and for all whom to follow: God or Baal.

And Elijah, on the top of Mount Carmel with his head between his knees... *waiting.*

Six times Elijah sent his servant to look to the Mediterranean Sea for a sign of rain. Six times the servant returned with nothing to report.

So Elijah sent him a seventh time, and the servant returned reporting a very small cloud rising from the sea.

It was the harbinger of rains.

LIKE ELIJAH, WE ARE WAITING IN PERILOUS TIMES.

We are waiting *to see Your promises fulfilled.*
We are waiting *for peace again on our city streets.*
We are waiting *for hardened hearts to turn back to You.*

AND MOST OF ALL, WE ARE WAITING FOR THE WORLD TO SEE YOUR GLORY RISING LIKE STEAM OVER THE SEA.

We are waiting for heaven's rains to saturate this dry place with grace.

And waiting for answers to our prayers. So we wait, Lord.

Lord, would you help us not to get distracted as we wait? Help us believe Your promises... even when the reports we hear are not good.

WE KEEP PRAYING—AND KEEP ASKING— SEVEN TIMES AND MORE!

We are watching and waiting until we see Your glory rising.
Until that day, in the name of Jesus, Amen!

Your Prayer:　　　Date:

Prayer answered:

DAY 23: STRONGER TOGETHER

WHILE MOSES HELD UP HIS HAND, ISRAEL PREVAILED, BUT WHENEVER HE PUT HIS HAND DOWN, AMALEK PREVAILED. WHEN MOSES' HANDS GREW HEAVY, THEY TOOK A STONE AND PUT IT UNDER HIM, AND HE SAT DOWN ON IT. THEN AARON AND HUR SUPPORTED HIS HANDS, ONE ON ONE SIDE AND ONE ON THE OTHER SO THAT HIS HANDS REMAINED STEADY UNTIL THE SUN WENT DOWN. SO JOSHUA DEFEATED AMALEK AND HIS ARMY WITH THE SWORD.

— EXODUS 17:11-13 (HCSB)

I'm so blessed, Lord.
I'm so blessed to know that I do not walk this journey alone. Blessed to know the friendship of other believers. Sharing life… together. Sharing prayers… together.

It's a mystery…

When we come together in Your Name—Jesus!—You are there in our midst. Think of that!

AGAIN, I ASSURE YOU: IF TWO OF YOU ON EARTH AGREE ABOUT ANY MATTER THAT YOU PRAY FOR, IT WILL BE DONE FOR YOU BY MY FATHER IN HEAVEN. FOR WHERE TWO OR THREE ARE GATHERED TOGETHER IN MY NAME, I AM THERE AMONG THEM."

— MATTHEW 18:19-20 (HCSB)

All of our differences—great and small—come together in You. One spiritual body with new meaning and purpose. Your arms and Your legs walking together in Heavenly strength, bringing Your Light to a world in need.

Lord, our scars, our experiences, our abundance and need, we'll always have enough because Your provision and love overflows!

NOW THE LARGE GROUP OF THOSE WHO BELIEVED WERE OF ONE HEART AND MIND, AND NO ONE SAID THAT ANY OF HIS POSSESSIONS WAS HIS OWN, BUT INSTEAD THEY HELD EVERYTHING IN COMMON.

— ACTS 4:32 (HCSB)

We are so blessed, Lord. But do we know it? Do we really understand what we have?

Forgive us, Lord, for forgetting.

Help us remember the selfless sacrifice You made so that we could truly be one, especially in perilous times:

I AM IN THEM AND YOU ARE IN ME. MAY THEY BE MADE COMPLETELY ONE, SO THE WORLD MAY KNOW YOU HAVE SENT ME AND HAVE LOVED THEM AS YOU HAVE LOVED ME.

— JOHN 17:23 (HCSB)

You gave Your life for all of us.

Lord, open our eyes to recognize our brothers and sisters—our everlasting family! Let's break bread together and lift our voices in praise, one mighty chorus of Hallelujahs rising to Your throne: Your children—at last!— together.

Making You smile.

Bring us together, so you may be lifted up, Jesus, and be the Light to a darkening world. Amen!

Your Prayer: Date:

Prayer answered:

DAY 24: WHO IS THE ENEMY?

FINALLY, BE STRONG IN THE LORD AND IN HIS MIGHTY POWER. PUT ON THE FULL ARMOR OF GOD, SO THAT YOU CAN TAKE YOUR STAND AGAINST THE DEVIL'S SCHEMES. FOR OUR STRUGGLE IS NOT AGAINST FLESH AND BLOOD, BUT AGAINST THE RULERS, AGAINST THE AUTHORITIES, AGAINST THE POWERS OF THIS DARK WORLD AND AGAINST THE SPIRITUAL FORCES OF EVIL IN THE HEAVENLY REALMS. THEREFORE PUT ON THE FULL ARMOR OF GOD, SO THAT WHEN THE DAY OF EVIL COMES, YOU MAY BE ABLE TO STAND YOUR GROUND, AND AFTER YOU HAVE DONE EVERYTHING, TO STAND.

— EPHESIANS 6:10-13 (NIV)

The one behind all of this hate, Lord... it's not who it seems.
Our enemy—the one who strikes matches of unrest and fans the flames of division—is hidden. He's the accuser of Your people and he deceives the world with lies.

But this is no surprise to us because Your word reveals the truth:

OUR ENEMY IS NOT FLESH AND BLOOD.

Lord, help us stand firm in the spiritual battle. Help us be strong in Your power alone.

You've given us special armor—spiritual armor— to take our stand against this unseen enemy. Your Word gives us Your battle plan for perilous times such as these:

> PUT ON THE FULL ARMOR OF GOD, SO THAT WHEN THE DAY OF EVIL COMES, YOU MAY BE ABLE TO STAND YOUR GROUND, AND AFTER YOU HAVE DONE EVERYTHING, TO STAND. STAND FIRM THEN, WITH THE BELT OF TRUTH BUCKLED AROUND YOUR WAIST, WITH THE BREASTPLATE OF RIGHTEOUSNESS IN PLACE, AND WITH YOUR FEET FITTED WITH THE READINESS THAT COMES FROM THE GOSPEL OF PEACE. IN ADDITION TO ALL THIS, TAKE UP THE SHIELD OF FAITH, WITH WHICH YOU CAN EXTINGUISH ALL THE FLAMING ARROWS OF THE EVIL ONE. TAKE THE HELMET OF SALVATION AND THE SWORD OF THE SPIRIT, WHICH IS THE WORD OF GOD.
>
> AND PRAY IN THE SPIRIT ON ALL OCCASIONS WITH ALL KINDS OF PRAYERS AND REQUESTS. WITH THIS IN MIND, BE ALERT AND ALWAYS KEEP ON PRAYING FOR ALL THE LORD'S PEOPLE.
>
> — EPHESIANS 6:11-18 (NIV)

Help us, then, to remember to wear your spiritual armor each day, and Lord, remind us to pray for each other because You answer.

After all, Lord, it's not our battle at all. It's Yours! And it's already won!

In the name of Jesus, Amen!

Your Prayer: Date:

_____

_____

_____

_____

_____

_____

_____

_____

_____

_____

_____

_____

_____

_____

_____

_____

_____

_____

_____

Prayer answered: _____

_____

_____

_____

DAY 25: TRUTH AND LIES

❧

When the Spirit of truth comes, He will guide you into all the truth. For He will not speak on His own, but He will speak whatever He hears. He will also declare to you what is to come.

— JOHN 16:13 (HCSB)

house of mirrors.
        That's what it's like living in this world, today, Lord. I see a multitude of reflections, and I'm not sure which one is real.

I watch one news anchor report a story, then flip the channel and hear the same event reported by someone else with a completely different angle. Which one is true?

It's hard to tell the facts from the spin right now. More than ever before, I need You to guide me in Truth.

Lord, help me discern the lies from the truth. Uncover the deceptions—one by one—and expose them in the Light.

Surround me in truth today:

> GIVE ME EARS TO HEAR IT.
> GIVE ME A STRONG VOICE TO SHARE IT.
> GIVE ME A HEART THAT YEARNS FOR IT.

Help me stay grounded in Your word each day, because Your Word is Truth. In knowing Christ, we can know Truth.

JESUS ANSWERED, "I AM THE WAY AND THE TRUTH AND THE LIFE. NO ONE COMES TO THE FATHER EXCEPT THROUGH ME.

— JOHN 14:6 (HCSB)

And truth will set us free:

So JESUS SAID TO THE JEWS WHO HAD BELIEVED HIM, "IF YOU CONTINUE IN MY WORD, YOU REALLY ARE MY DISCIPLES. YOU WILL KNOW THE TRUTH, AND THE TRUTH WILL SET YOU FREE."

— JOHN 8:31-32 (HCSB)

Likewise, Lord, guard my mouth against speaking untruths. May I speak the truth in love when needed, and when it is spoken to me, give me ears hear it.

BUT SPEAKING THE TRUTH IN LOVE, LET US GROW IN EVERY WAY INTO HIM WHO IS THE HEAD—CHRIST.

— EPHESIANS 4:15 (HCSB)

Your Word says:

I'VE WRITTEN TO WARN YOU ABOUT THOSE WHO ARE TRYING TO DECEIVE

YOU. BUT THEY'RE NO MATCH FOR WHAT IS EMBEDDED DEEPLY WITHIN YOU—CHRIST'S ANOINTING, NO LESS! YOU DON'T NEED ANY OF THEIR SO-CALLED TEACHING. CHRIST'S ANOINTING TEACHES YOU THE TRUTH ON EVERYTHING YOU NEED TO KNOW ABOUT YOURSELF AND HIM, UNCONTAMINATED BY A SINGLE LIE. LIVE DEEPLY IN WHAT YOU WERE TAUGHT.

— 1 JOHN 2:26-27 (MSG)

Lord, let me live in Truth today. Especially in perilous times!

I ask these things in the name of Jesus, the Way the Truth and the Life, Amen!

Your Prayer: Date:

_____

_____

_____

_____

_____

_____

_____

_____

_____

_____

_____

_____

_____

_____

_____

_____

_____

_____

_____

Prayer answered:

_____

_____

_____

DAY 26: REMEMBER TO DANCE

A TIME TO WEEP AND A TIME TO LAUGH, A TIME TO MOURN AND A TIME TO DANCE...

— ECCLESIASTES 3:4 NIV

I sometimes *forget to dance, Lord.* To sing out loud and lift my face to the sun's warmth, remembering that You are good!

Your word says:

SO IN CHRIST JESUS YOU ARE ALL CHILDREN OF GOD THROUGH FAITH, FOR ALL OF YOU WHO WERE BAPTIZED INTO CHRIST HAVE CLOTHED YOURSELVES WITH CHRIST.

— GALATIANS 3:26-27 (NIV)

What Father, then, wants to see His children live as defeated? Especially when we are not!

In Christ, we are victorious:

But thanks be to God! He gives us the victory through our Lord Jesus Christ.

— 1 CORINTHIANS 15:57 (NIV)

In Christ, we have strength to do everything we are called to do:

I can do all this through him who gives me strength.

— PHILIPPIANS 4:13 (NIV)

We are never alone in the battle, for You, Lord, have promised to be with us and even to fight for us:

For the Lord your God is the one who goes with you to fight for you against your enemies to give you victory.

— DEUTERONOMY 20:4 (NIV)

Our Messiah has overcome the world, even death!

Where, O death, is your victory? Where, O death, is your sting?

— 1 CORINTHIANS 15:55 (NIV)

So yes! I will dance! I'll shout and sing! I declare this day to be the Lord's! I will rejoice and be glad!

I'll remember that the Lord is my strength and my song! I will say:

"The Lord is good!

The Lord is good!
The Lord is good!"

And I'll dance and sing like King David before the Lord… especially in this perilous time:

DAVID'S SONG OF PRAISE:

> GIVE THANKS TO THE LORD, FOR HE IS GOOD; HIS LOVE ENDURES FOREVER. CRY OUT, "SAVE US, GOD OUR SAVIOR; GATHER US AND DELIVER US FROM THE NATIONS, THAT WE MAY GIVE THANKS TO YOUR HOLY NAME, AND GLORY IN YOUR PRAISE."

— 1 CHRONICLES 16:34-35 (NIV)

Praise to you, Jesus, Who goes before me! Amen!

Your Prayer: Date:

Prayer answered:

DAY 27: PRAYING SCRIPTURE IN PERILOUS TIMES

For no matter how many promises God has made, they are "Yes" in Christ. And so through him the "Amen" is spoken by us to the glory of God.

— 2 CORINTHIANS 1:20 (NIV)

---

ord, I come to You now in prayer agreeing with Your Word and the promises that it contains.

You are faithful to Your Word, including each of the powerful promises found in Psalm 91. Lord, remember these promises in this perilous time:

Whoever dwells in the shelter of the Most High will rest in the shadow of the Almighty. I will say of the Lord, "He is my refuge and my fortress, my God, in whom I trust."

— PSALM 91:1-2 (NIV)

Father, I rest in Your shelter.

SURELY HE WILL SAVE YOU FROM THE FOWLER'S SNARE AND FROM THE DEADLY PESTILENCE.

HE WILL COVER YOU WITH HIS FEATHERS, AND UNDER HIS WINGS YOU WILL FIND REFUGE; HIS FAITHFULNESS WILL BE YOUR SHIELD AND RAMPART.

— PSLAM 91:3-4 (NIV)

Father, you have promised to save me, protect me, and be my shield.

YOU WILL NOT FEAR THE TERROR OF NIGHT, NOR THE ARROW THAT FLIES BY DAY, NOR THE PESTILENCE THAT STALKS IN THE DARKNESS, NOR THE PLAGUE THAT DESTROYS AT MIDDAY.

A THOUSAND MAY FALL AT YOUR SIDE, TEN THOUSAND AT YOUR RIGHT HAND, BUT IT WILL NOT COME NEAR YOU.

YOU WILL ONLY OBSERVE WITH YOUR EYES AND SEE THE PUNISHMENT OF THE WICKED.

— PSALM 91:5-8 (NIV)

I will fear no evil, for You protect me.

IF YOU SAY, "THE LORD IS MY REFUGE," AND YOU MAKE THE MOST HIGH YOUR DWELLING, NO HARM WILL OVERTAKE YOU, NO DISASTER WILL COME NEAR YOUR TENT.

FOR HE WILL COMMAND HIS ANGELS CONCERNING YOU TO GUARD YOU IN ALL YOUR WAYS; THEY WILL LIFT YOU UP IN THEIR HANDS, SO THAT YOU WILL NOT STRIKE YOUR FOOT AGAINST A STONE.

YOU WILL TREAD ON THE LION AND THE COBRA; YOU WILL TRAMPLE THE GREAT LION AND THE SERPENT.

— PSALM 91:9-13

Lord, You are my refuge! I trust You completely. I live and breathe in Your divine care.

"BECAUSE HE LOVES ME," SAYS THE LORD, "I WILL RESCUE HIM; I WILL PROTECT HIM, FOR HE ACKNOWLEDGES MY NAME.

HE WILL CALL ON ME, AND I WILL ANSWER HIM; I WILL BE WITH HIM IN TROUBLE, I WILL DELIVER HIM AND HONOR HIM.

WITH LONG LIFE I WILL SATISFY HIM AND SHOW HIM MY SALVATION."

I call on You now, Lord, to rescue me in this perilous time! I know you are with me, though the world seems upside-down and confused. Even so, Lord, You are my honor and I love You.

In the name of Your precious Son, Jesus, Amen!

Your Prayer:

Date:

_____

_____

_____

_____

_____

_____

_____

_____

_____

_____

_____

_____

_____

_____

_____

_____

_____

_____

_____

_____

Prayer answered:

_____

_____

_____

DAY 28: RIGHTEOUSNESS IN PERILOUS TIMES

Be alert and of sober mind. Your enemy the devil prowls around like a roaring lion looking for someone to devour.

—1 PETER 5:8 (NIV)

In a minefield, the enemy sets hidden traps.
You don't see them, of course. The traps are cleverly buried underground, lying in wait for one wrong step. A meandering walk might kill you in a minefield.

MAYBE THAT'S WHY YOU CALL US TO LIVE HOLY LIVES... TO AVOID LANDMINES BY WALKING A STRAIGHT PATH.

Your Word tells us to "put on righteousness" in battle. Yet, Lord, I'm still learning about righteousness.

Righteousness is *given to me by Christ* to cover my heart like armor. *This is the righteousness that assures me of my salvation.*

But there's more, isn't there? There is something about right-eousness that I'm just beginning to understand:

When You call me to put on righteousness, You are calling me to live a holy life. You are calling me to walk a straight path.

YOU ALSO TELL ME THAT I HAVE AN ACCUSER. AND HE WANTS TO BRING ME DOWN.

Oh, he can't keep me out of heaven— Jesus purchased that ticket! The enemy will never snatch me from Your hand:

I GIVE THEM ETERNAL LIFE, AND THEY SHALL NEVER PERISH; NO ONE WILL SNATCH THEM OUT OF MY HAND.

— JOHN 10:28 (NIV)

But he is hungry to destroy, and prowling, ready to attack! He pollutes the world with confusion and poisons it with corruption. This world is brimming with both. Given the chance, he'd steal my peace and joy. He's waiting to call me out.

So why give him the chance?

Oh, I know, Lord, there's sin in my life. I need your grace every day! And your mercies? They are new each morning!

No, I'm not perfect, but this is what I desire: to *press on* to be all that Christ calls me to be:

NOT THAT I HAVE ALREADY OBTAINED ALL THIS, OR HAVE ALREADY ARRIVED AT MY GOAL, BUT I PRESS ON TO TAKE HOLD OF THAT FOR WHICH CHRIST JESUS TOOK HOLD OF ME. BROTHERS AND SISTERS, I DO NOT CONSIDER MYSELF YET TO HAVE TAKEN HOLD OF IT. BUT ONE THING I DO: FORGETTING WHAT IS BEHIND AND STRAINING TOWARD WHAT IS AHEAD, I PRESS ON TOWARD THE GOAL TO WIN THE PRIZE FOR WHICH GOD HAS CALLED ME HEAVENWARD IN CHRIST JESUS.

— PHILIPPIANS 3:12-14 (NIV)

To strive for more of your holiness in my life... especially in this battle! It's a struggle that will only end the day I see Your face.

IN THIS PERILOUS TIME, SHOW ME THE AREAS IN MY LIFE THAT ARE VULNERABLE TO SIN.

Help me take my Christian walk seriously! Don't let me meander my way through life risking attack. Help me, Lord, to walk a straight path and avoid any landmines that will maim my Christian walk.

Most of all, Lord, thank you for the righteousness of Jesus that completely covers my sin. He sets the model for all you call me to be.

BLESSED ARE THOSE WHO HUNGER AND THIRST FOR RIGHTEOUSNESS, FOR THEY WILL BE FILLED.

— MATTHEW 5:6 (NIV)

I ask these things in the name of Jesus, Amen!

Your Prayer: Date:

_____

_____

_____

_____

_____

_____

_____

_____

_____

_____

_____

_____

_____

_____

_____

_____

_____

Prayer answered:

_____

_____

_____

DAY 29: JUST BE

Lord, I love the house where you live, the place where your glory dwells.

— PSALM 26:8 (NIV)

---

*S*ometimes *I make it harder than it has to be.*

The countless studies and piles of books. The endless documentaries and discussions. These are all good things, but they are never enough.

So I over-analyze and ponder until my head hurts. I write and talk and write some more.

In all of this striving to know You more, I can miss the point entirely.

You simply call me to be with You. To sit quietly in Your presence ... and listen.

It's so simple that it's hard to me, doing the simplest thing!

This culture thrives on doing. Work more! Be smarter! Try harder! And it's never enough, is it?

And You?

You ask me to sit at Your feet for a while and listen. You ask me to just... be.

I don't have to impress anyone at all. *That's such a freeing concept!*

I don't have to know all of the answers—*because You do.*

I will never have to pretend to be what I am not—*because You love me for who I am.*

How refreshing to be accepted unconditionally... especially in this culture!

So I'll just be.

I'll be with You and I'll listen to You.

In this perilous time, Your Word contains wisdom, and it's there for the taking. I'll sit with the Bible on my lap and let Your Words seep deeply into my soul.

I'll listen and simply be me.

"Martha, Martha," the Lord answered, "you are worried and upset about many things, but few things are needed—or indeed only one. Mary has chosen what is better, and it will not be taken away from her."

— LUKE 10:41–42 (NIV)

Thank you for loving me just as I am, Jesus, Amen!

Your Prayer: Date:

_____

_____

_____

_____

_____

_____

_____

_____

_____

_____

_____

_____

_____

_____

_____

_____

_____

_____

Prayer answered:

_____

_____

_____

DAY 30: A POWERFUL PRAYER IN THESE THREE WORDS

⁂

HE WHO DWELLS IN THE SHELTER OF THE MOST HIGH WILL REMAIN SECURE AND REST IN THE SHADOW OF THE ALMIGHTY [WHOSE POWER NO ENEMY CAN WITHSTAND].

I WILL SAY OF THE LORD, "HE IS MY REFUGE AND MY FORTRESS, MY GOD, IN WHOM I TRUST [WITH GREAT CONFIDENCE, AND ON WHOM I RELY]!"

— PSALM 91:1-2 (AMP)

*T*hree words.

Whenever I face obstacles too great to overcome, or when the enemy is knocking at my door, I pray three words, Lord. *Three.*

And now I come to You to pray for our nation, and I don't even know where to begin. Everywhere I look, there's division. Overseas, rumors of wars abound.

In the schools, in the markets, even on our streets. It's all the same: confusion and uncertainty.

And I am unsettled.

So I run to my place of peace and I get down on my knees and I pray the only prayer I know that gives me peace:

I TRUST YOU.

The future is uncertain and I'm not sure our nation can be whole again.

BUT, LORD, I TRUST YOU.

When I'm overwhelmed and weary, or when I don't have enough time or resources—and my faith seems so very small— these three words are all that I need, Lord:

I TRUST YOU.

You will keep the mind that is dependent on You in perfect peace, for it is trusting in You:

YOU WILL KEEP THE MIND THAT IS DEPENDENT ON YOU IN PERFECT PEACE, FOR IT IS TRUSTING IN YOU.

— ISAIAH 26:3 (HCSB)

Whenever I am afraid, Jesus, I will trust in You. Amen!

Your Prayer: Date:

Prayer answered:

DAY 31: THE OUTSIDER

LET'S GO OUTSIDE, WHERE JESUS IS, WHERE THE ACTION IS—NOT TRYING TO BE PRIVILEGED INSIDERS, BUT TAKING OUR SHARE IN THE ABUSE OF JESUS. THIS "INSIDER WORLD" IS NOT OUR HOME. WE HAVE OUR EYES PEELED FOR THE CITY ABOUT TO COME.

— HEBREWS 13:13-14 (MSG)

*I*nsiders.

That's the buzzword in the media right now. It describes people who take high positions to help others but in reality think only of themselves.

Maybe they started with good intentions, but somehow they forgot about the people whose hands they shook along the way. They entered and closed the doors behind them.

And we are angry. Lord, I am angry.

It's true. There's an "insider club" where most of us will never be invited. If you're in, you dine at formal tables on China plates filled with gourmet foods—while the people outside feast on empty promises.

Lord, I confess that I'm weary of watching the insiders take without giving. I'm so tired of being left out. I confess: I'm angry!

BUT THEN I THINK OF YOU, JESUS. YOU LEFT A HEAVENLY THRONE —A PLACE OF HONOR—AND BECAME AN OUTSIDER.

So how can I demand a place with the insiders, when You slept where the livestock ate discarded scraps?

From the day of Your birth, when sweet Mary and Joseph couldn't get a room, to Your lonely death outside of the Jerusalem gates: *You were the Outsider.*

You did what was needed to reach us. You became an Outsider to know our pain and our anguish firsthand.

YOU BECAME ONE OF US.

In a world of privilege and self-centeredness, You were different.

Today, corruption rules and golden gates are erected to keep us out. Empty promises are made to everyday folk who watch their dreams fade away, a little more each year.

In this perilous time, You call us to be like you. You call us to be different, too.

You call us to go outside of the city gates—where the thieves roam and the tears fall and sorrows abound—because this is the place where Love flowed down.

TRUE BEAUTY AND POWER ARE FOUND OUTSIDE OF THE GATES WITH YOU. AND THE SECRET? EVERYONE IS INVITED THERE WITH YOU.

No, I can't be angry when this is not my home. My home is beyond that heavenly gate.

My home... is with You.

BUT THERE'S FAR MORE TO LIFE FOR US. WE'RE CITIZENS OF HIGH HEAVEN! WE'RE WAITING THE ARRIVAL OF THE SAVIOR, THE MASTER, JESUS CHRIST, WHO WILL TRANSFORM OUR EARTHY BODIES INTO GLORIOUS BODIES LIKE HIS OWN. HE'LL MAKE US BEAUTIFUL AND WHOLE WITH THE SAME POWERFUL SKILL BY WHICH HE IS PUTTING EVERYTHING AS IT SHOULD BE, UNDER AND AROUND HIM.

— PHILIPPIANS 3:20-21 (MSG)

Thank You, Lord Jesus, for making us citizens of a heavenly home. Amen!

Your Prayer: Date:

_____

_____

_____

_____

_____

_____

_____

_____

_____

_____

_____

_____

_____

_____

_____

_____

_____

_____

_____

_____

Prayer answered:

_____

_____

_____

_____

DAY 32: ENCOURAGED BY PROPHECY

REMEMBER THE FORMER THINGS, THOSE OF LONG AGO; I AM GOD, AND
THERE IS NO OTHER; I AM GOD, AND THERE IS NONE LIKE ME. I MAKE
KNOWN THE END FROM THE BEGINNING, FROM ANCIENT TIMES, WHAT IS
STILL TO COME. I SAY, 'MY PURPOSE WILL STAND, AND I WILL DO ALL
THAT I PLEASE.

— ISAIAH 46:9-10 (NIV)

*From the beginning, You declare the end.
Ours is an epic tale, God:*

*An awe-inspiring creation.
A catastrophic fall.
A jaw-dropping redemption.*

A story with a thrilling climax that leaves us breathless. And
it's all there, written down for us in Scripture.

You've shared it with us—the end from the beginning.

Some live by a watch and others scribble dates in a planner. We try as best we can to master the minutes and days and years of our lives. Even so, time gets the best of us.

But You?

You master time, and it has no hold on You!

So why not study the signs You've given us in Your word? Penned by many authors years apart— One message: *Redemption.* The scoffers say, "Where is this coming? It's always the same."

First off, you need to know that in the last days, mockers are going to have a heyday. Reducing everything to the level of their puny feelings, they'll mock, "So what's happened to the promise of his Coming? Our ancestors are dead and buried, and everything's going on just as it has from the first day of creation. Nothing's changed."

— 2 PETER 3:3-4 (MSG)

But they've forgotten Your faithfulness that proves Your promises true.

Some are alarmed by your prophecies, and I understand. I've been unnerved, too, but no more!

Now I'm encouraged by prophecy in your Word. you have declared the victory ahead. We win!

Jesus admonished the Pharisees and Sadducees when He said:

"When evening comes, you say, 'It will be fair weather, for the sky is red,' and in the morning, 'Today it will be stormy, for the

SKY IS RED AND OVERCAST.' YOU KNOW HOW TO INTERPRET THE
APPEARANCE OF THE SKY, BUT YOU CANNOT INTERPRET THE SIGNS OF
THE TIMES."

— MATTHEW 16:2-3 (NIV)

Buds form on branches and leaves turn to flame to signal a new season. Light breaks the night sky as dawn approaches. The sun glows red as evening falls.

The leaves of the silver maple turn their undersides to the sky when the rain is about to fall.

IF WE LOOK, THE SIGNS ARE THERE. YOUR WORDS OF PROPHECY ENCOURAGE ME IN PERILOUS TIMES.

So let them say the world is falling apart. Let them say the corruption will be our undoing. Or that our hope is in the hands of a politician, and we'll never find peace again.

BUT I HAVE READ YOUR PROPHECIES, AND I WON'T BE DECEIVED.

Oh, God! That the hearts of Your people would yearn to learn Your word! That we would once again declare these verses from our pulpits, teaching the people to be encouraged— not dismayed!

Oh, God! That You would pull away the veil so we would understand in Your perfect timing.

THEN WE WILL BE READY, WAITING FOR YOU WITH PLENTY OF OIL.

I'm taking my eyes off of this world's woes and focusing instead on the sky. I'm watching and waiting for you, Jesus!

WHEN THESE THINGS BEGIN TO TAKE PLACE, STAND UP AND LIFT UP YOUR
HEADS, BECAUSE YOUR REDEMPTION IS DRAWING NEAR.

— LUKE 21:28 (NIV)

Yes, come, Lord Jesus, come! Amen!

Your Prayer: Date:

Prayer answered:

DAY 33: THE SECRET ARMY

BUT SINCE WE BELONG TO THE DAY, LET US BE SOBER, PUTTING ON FAITH AND LOVE AS A BREASTPLATE, AND THE HOPE OF SALVATION AS A HELMET. FOR GOD DID NOT APPOINT US TO SUFFER WRATH BUT TO RECEIVE SALVATION THROUGH OUR LORD JESUS CHRIST.

— 1 THESSALONIANS 5:8-9 (NIV)

There exists a secret army.
They live quietly without drawing attention to themselves. Sometimes in prayer closets, sometimes blended into a crowd.

They may be sitting at a kitchen table with a neighbor or walking down a street. Prayer warriors... silently asking that Your will be done.

Some pray alone, others hold a hand or two. Fathers and sons, mothers and daughters, grandparents and neighbors.

THESE ARE YOUR PEOPLE, LORD. YOUR SECRET ARMY.

The world does not recognize these soldiers. They live without fame or special honors, but this is not their goal. Most overlook them, but You see them, Lord!

THEY DO NOT DRAW ATTENTION TO THEMSELVES BECAUSE THEIR HEARTS ARE SET APART FOR YOU.

In days of plenty, they lift praises to You. In perilous times, though, their faith grows like a Lenten rose in the snow.

Persecution is but a catalyst for prayers that fly to the heavens and usher in Your mighty hand. The world pushes hard against Your people, yet Your people prevail!

Hard-pressed but not crushed—perplexed but not in despair, prayers rising to Your throne—even now!

Your church is around us, every day. The gates of hell will never bring it down!

Sometimes I pass a person on the street, and the Spirit quickens, a recognition of a brother or sister, one of the body of Christ.

A SECRET WARRIOR.

Sometimes, Lord, we feel so alone. Remind us, then, that we are not.

OLD, YOUNG, MARRIED, SINGLE, MAN, WOMAN… WE ARE OUT THERE, PRAYING FOR YOUR WILL TO BE DONE IN HEAVEN AND ON EARTH.

So be it, Lord! Call us to our God-given posts, always in prayer and in Your word, standing firm on Your precious promises.

BUT WHEN YOU PRAY, GO INTO YOUR ROOM, CLOSE THE DOOR AND PRAY TO YOUR FATHER, WHO IS UNSEEN. THEN YOUR FATHER, WHO SEES WHAT IS DONE IN SECRET, WILL REWARD YOU.

— MATTHEW 6:6 (NIV)

For Yours is the kingdom, the power, and glory, Amen!

Your Prayer: Date:

Prayer answered:

DAY 34: DARKNESS AND LIGHT

You are the light of the world. A city situated on a hill cannot be hidden. No one lights a lamp and puts it under a basket, but rather on a lampstand, and it gives light for all who are in the house.

— MATTHEW 5:14-15 (HCSB)

*I*t's the age-old battle, God, as it was in the beginning of time —darkness and Light.

The earth was dark, without form and empty. It was covered in a darkness unlike anything we know of today. A complete blackout. *Until You called for Light, and Light chased the darkness away.*

I can imagine You there, Lord, hovering over the darkness. *Waiting.*

I can imagine the sound of Your thunderous voice calling forth Light.

ONE WORD—LIGHT!—AND THE DARKNESS FLED.

It still does.

I can imagine the heavens—an inky blackness—until Your word set lights in the sky with astounding precision to give order to man's days, and to mark appointed times and seasons:

> AND GOD SAID, "LET THERE BE LIGHTS IN THE VAULT OF THE SKY TO SEPARATE THE DAY FROM THE NIGHT, AND LET THEM SERVE AS SIGNS TO MARK SACRED TIMES, AND DAYS AND YEARS, AND LET THEM BE LIGHTS IN THE VAULT OF THE SKY TO GIVE LIGHT ON THE EARTH." AND IT WAS SO.
>
> — GENESIS 1:14-15 (NIV)

You gave stars to be lights in the darkness, even signals to mark seasons! Even now, You call us out into the darkness —Be Light!

When the darkness is like a thick blanket—like a night without stars or moonlight—I know You are there, waiting. *Hovering.* Until we do what we were created to do—to be Your Light.

So today, Lord, this is my prayer:

HELP ME BE A LIGHT IN THE DARKNESS. GIVE ME THE COURAGE TO LET YOUR LIGHT SHINE WITHIN ME.

You, Sweet Jesus, are the Light of the world! When You are lifted up—even now—the darkness will flee! As the moon reflects the sun's light, we are to reflect the Son's Light.

HOW AMAZING IS THAT? WE WERE CREATED TO SHINE.

Lord, would You take away anything that hinders Your Light in my life? Help me be the Light that You called me to be.

Especially in these perilous times.

WHEN JESUS SPOKE AGAIN TO THE PEOPLE, HE SAID, "I AM THE LIGHT OF THE WORLD. WHOEVER FOLLOWS ME WILL NEVER WALK IN DARKNESS, BUT WILL HAVE THE LIGHT OF LIFE."

— JOHN 8:12 (NIV)

Thank you, Jesus, for being the Light to my life, and to this world. Amen!

Your Prayer: Date:

Prayer answered:

DAY 35: DON'T GIVE UP

LET US NOT GROW WEARY OR BECOME DISCOURAGED IN DOING GOOD,
FOR AT THE PROPER TIME WE WILL REAP, IF WE DO NOT GIVE IN.

— GALATIANS 6:9 (AMP)

ight now, Lord, I'm tired.
The summer is hot and dry and our emotions are on edge. We're tired of politics and debt and disagreements and anger. Tired of trying to be more and do more and get ahead.

It's like trying to hold back the tide in the middle of a storm.

The enemy wants to *wear us out.* He wants us to *lose heart and walk away defeated,* and to *doubt that our drawn-out summer will ever end.*

HE WILL SPEAK WORDS AGAINST THE MOST HIGH [GOD] AND WEAR
DOWN THE SAINTS OF THE MOST HIGH, AND HE WILL INTEND TO
CHANGE THE TIMES AND THE LAW; AND THEY WILL BE GIVEN INTO HIS

HAND FOR A TIME, [TWO] TIMES, AND HALF A TIME [THREE AND ONE-HALF YEARS].

— DANIEL 7:25 (AMP)

Oppression hangs in the air like humidity. The heat lingers—I can't get away from it. I'm longing for the autumn to come and break this oppressive heat.

OH, BRING THE HARVEST, LORD! WE ARE WAITING TO SEE IT COME IN. WE LONG TO BE REFRESHED AGAIN!

Tomorrow is another day, another prayer, another sigh.

STRENGTHEN, ME, LORD, TO BE PERSISTENT IN PRAYER IN THIS PERILOUS TIME. HELP ME TO PRAY WHEN THE HARVEST IS DELAYED. I REFUSE TO LET GO OF FAITH!

I know that You have a plan—and it's for our good! So I'll keep asking, Lord:

> *Restore our nation, and heal our land.*
> *But most importantly, turn our hearts back to You!*
> *Bring the harvest, Lord! We are waiting!*

SO WHAT MAKES YOU THINK GOD WON'T STEP IN AND WORK JUSTICE FOR HIS CHOSEN PEOPLE, WHO CONTINUE TO CRY OUT FOR HELP? WON'T HE STICK UP FOR THEM? I ASSURE YOU, HE WILL. HE WILL NOT DRAG HIS FEET. BUT HOW MUCH OF THAT KIND OF PERSISTENT FAITH WILL THE SON OF MAN FIND ON THE EARTH WHEN HE RETURNS?"

— LUKE 18:6-8 (MSG)

In the name of Jesus, Amen!

Your Prayer: Date:

Prayer answered:

DAY 36: KNOW HIS VOICE

THE GATEKEEPER OPENS THE GATE FOR HIM, AND THE SHEEP LISTEN TO HIS VOICE. HE CALLS HIS OWN SHEEP BY NAME AND LEADS THEM OUT.

— JOHN 10:3 (NIV)

I want to know Your voice, Jesus. Really know it!
There are countless voices in the world today, telling me to do this or to believe that. With so much noise, Lord, help me hear Your voice clearly each day. To recognize Your voice in this chaotic world.

YOUR WORD IS THE KEY TO KNOWING YOUR VOICE BECAUSE IT TEACHES ME YOUR WAYS.

The more I read it, Jesus, the more I know Your voice. It rises above the noise and *speaks life*.

Yet there's another voice out there—and it would lead me astray.

Our enemy has a voice, too, and his lies never change. He has a distinct modus operandi, but Your Word teaches us to recognize it. I am so thankful that Your Word teaches us how to discern the enemy's voice.

How great the difference between the two:

You advocate for us!
The enemy accuses us.

You speak only Truth.
The enemy deceives. He's the father of lies.

Your voice brings us into Light.
The enemy's voice leads us into darkness.

Your voice teaches concern for others.
The enemy's words are always self-centered.

You love God's Word and remind us of it.
The enemy detracts from Scripture.

You speak in a still small voice.
The enemy shouts.

Your voice brings us closer together.
The enemy seeks to push us apart.

You patiently wait for us to listen.
The enemy invades our space, demanding to be heard.

Your words are gentle.
The enemy is pushy.

Your instruction leads to a sound mind.

The enemy leads to confusion.

Your words are patient.
The enemy wants to rush us into a decision.

Your words always agree with Scripture.
The enemy twists Scripture and begs us to doubt it.

Your words are full of hope.
The enemy speaks of hopelessness.

Your voice is always encouraging.
The enemy is critical and condemning.

MOST IMPORTANTLY, JESUS, YOUR VOICE LEADS TO EVERLASTING LIFE. THE ENEMY'S VOICE LEADS ONLY TO DEATH.

In this perilous time, Jesus, help me recognize both voices, so I will only follow the voice that leads to life.

BY THIS YOU KNOW AND RECOGNIZE THE SPIRIT OF GOD: EVERY SPIRIT THAT ACKNOWLEDGES AND CONFESSES [THE FACT] THAT JESUS CHRIST HAS [ACTUALLY] COME IN THE FLESH [AS A MAN] IS FROM GOD [GOD IS ITS SOURCE].

— 1 JOHN 4:2 (AMP)

May I know your voice and follow it always, Jesus, Amen!

Your Prayer: Date:

Prayer answered:

DAY 37: DIVINE WEAPONRY

Be prepared. You're up against far more than you can handle on your own. Take all the help you can get, every weapon God has issued, so that when it's all over but the shouting you'll still be on your feet.

— EPHESIANS 6:13 (MSG)

How do we fight a spiritual war, Lord?
Because our nation is in the midst of one now—*a spiritual war.*

A war that rages behind the events we see every day in the news. Behind the bombings and the terrorist attacks. Behind the riots and the coldness descending:

For our struggle is not against flesh and blood, but against the rulers, against the authorities, against the powers of this dark world and against the spiritual forces of evil in the heavenly realms.

— EPHESIANS 6:12 (NIV)

The battle is hidden from our eyes—but it is as real as the air we breathe. We've lost serious ground, Lord! It's time to fight.

Wake us up! Call us to arms! Sound the battle cry and ready us to fight this war!

LET US PUT ON *DIVINE WEAPONRY*—THE ONLY KIND TO WITHSTAND THIS SPIRITUAL WAR—AND FIGHT LIKE DAVID IN THE BATTLE OF OUR LIVES.

The only way to win this one is if we fight the battle Your way —with spiritual armor—so we will stand strong in Your power!

We are **belted in Your truth** so we will not be deceived!

Our hearts are protected by the **breastplate of the righteousness** that we wear in Christ!

Our **feet are fitted to be sure and steadfast with the gospel of peace**—the "good news"—of Christ, the Son of God who died to give us eternal life. This good news brings real peace—even in the midst of war!

We are protected by our **shield of faith** and will not let it go! It is our protection from the attacks of the enemy.

Our minds are guarded with **the helmet of salvation**, protecting us from deception. We know who we are—*redeemed by Christ as children and heirs of The Most High God*—no matter what the world says of us.

And lastly, we take up **the sword— the Word of God**. Bring it to our minds, Lord. Renew it in our hearts each day. This is our offensive weapon. Give us the strength to lift it up confidently!

And we pray without ceasing. We pray consistent prayers for the soul of our nation and for Israel. Prayers that rise to the very throne of God. We will not stop praying, Lord, until You answer.

Help us stay alert in this perilous time. We will see the victory, for this is Your promise:

> FOR I AM CONVINCED THAT NEITHER DEATH NOR LIFE, NEITHER ANGELS NOR DEMONS, NEITHER THE PRESENT NOR THE FUTURE, NOR ANY POWERS, NEITHER HEIGHT NOR DEPTH, NOR ANYTHING ELSE IN ALL CREATION, WILL BE ABLE TO SEPARATE US FROM THE LOVE OF GOD THAT IS IN CHRIST JESUS OUR LORD.
>
> — ROMANS 8:38-39 (NIV)

Thank you, Jesus, for the victory is won! Amen!

Your Prayer: Date:

Prayer answered:

DAY 38: THE MYSTERY OF GRATITUDE IN PRAYER

Rejoice always and delight in your faith; be unceasing and persistent in prayer; In every situation [no matter what the circumstances] be thankful and continually give thanks to God; for this is the will of God for you in Christ Jesus.

— 1 THESSALONIANS 5:16-18 (AMP)

---

*W*hy thankfulness? It baffles me, Lord.
Why does an eternal God—so great and mighty —desire gratitude from someone so ordinary?
And why do You say:

Don't worry about anything, but in everything, through prayer and petition with thanksgiving, let your requests be made known to God.

— PHILIPPIANS 4:6 (HCSB)

Thanksgiving, Lord? In a perilous time? Yet even now, with so much uncertain, You call me to *give thanks*.

THERE'S SOMETHING UNIQUELY PERSONAL ABOUT COMING TO YOU IN THANKFULNESS. WHEN I THINK OF ALL YOU'VE GIVEN ME, I AM AWARE OF YOUR PRESENCE.

Suddenly, You are there in my prayer room, lifting my chin so I see only You. Everything else fades away.

In this attitude of thankfulness, *I lean into You.*

In gratitude, *I draw closer.*

In that closeness, I whisper my prayers *and You hear them.*

Oh, my earthly eyes cannot see You leaning in to hear my requests, but when I come to you with an appreciation of Your many gifts—even the simplest gift like the air that fills my lungs —*my spirit knows You are here.*

YOU ARE PRESENT. I JUST KNOW.

See, I had it wrong. You don't need my gratitude at all. I'm the one in need. I need to recognize Your hand in my life. To stop awhile and become aware that I am, indeed, loved by You.

What more is there to say, knowing this? *I am loved.*

When I give thanks, Your love flows into the deepest parts of my aching soul.

AND NOTHING—NO WANT OR NEED, NO HURT OR SORROW— NOTHING STANDS IN THE WAY OF MY FATHER'S GREAT LOVE FOR ME.

Gratitude is fresh rain falling on the driest parts of my life. It prepares the soil for the miracles of new growth.

I'm so thankful, Lord that You have shown this to me today. I'm so very thankful for Your amazing love.

My soul, praise Yahweh, and all that is within me, praise His holy name.

My soul, praise the Lord, and do not forget all His benefits.

He forgives all your sin; He heals all your diseases.

He redeems your life from the Pit; He crowns you with faithful love and compassion.

He satisfies you with goodness; your youth is renewed like the eagle.

— PSALM 103:1-5 (HCSB)

Thank you, Father, for your never-ending love for me, Amen!

Your Prayer: Date:

Prayer answered:

DAY 39: WHY 40 PRAYERS?

You are my help and my deliverer; you are my God, do not delay.

— PSALM 40:17 (NIV)

---

4 0 *prayers.*

That's what You wanted. I didn't ponder the number… I just knew it was 40.

40 prayers to write. 40 urgent requests in a perilous time.

The question is…why 40? Why not 20? Or 10?

I searched Your Word for 40 and I found it there, often in perilous times:

You filled the earth with rains that cleansed the earth from evil in 40 days and 40 nights. (Genesis 7:12)

You directed Noah to release a raven and a dove 40 days after mountains peaks were seen above the waters. (Genesis 8:5-7)

You fed the Israelites manna in the wilderness for 40 years. (Exodus 16:35)

Moses spent 40 days and nights meeting with You on Mount Sinai... twice. (Exodus 24:18 and Exodus 34:27-28)

Spies scouted the Promised Land for 40 days. (Numbers 13:25 and Numbers 14:34)

You sent Jonah to warn the Ninevites that they had 40 days to repent, or judgment would fall. (Jonah 3:4)

Goliath taunted and tormented the Israelites for 40 days before David defeated him. (1 Samuel 17:16)

Elijah fled from Jezebel and journeyed 40 days and 40 nights to meet You on Mount Horeb. (1 Kings 19:8)

When Israel turned from Your ways, You gave them to suffer under the hand of the Philistines for 40 years until Samson delivered them. (Judges 13:1)

Jesus fasted and was tempted for 40 days and nights in the desert, and then started His saving ministry. (Matthew 4:2)

40 days passed between the resurrection of Jesus and His ascension (Acts 1:3)

You form us in the womb in 40 weeks.

In the 40th chapter of Exodus, Your Glory filled the Tabernacle. (Exodus 40:34)

So I give you 40 Prayers:

40 prayers to cry out to You in a time of great trial.
40 prayers to cleanse our hearts.
40 prayers to seek direction when we have lost our way.
40 prayers to heed Your warnings for You are a just God.
40 prayers to ask that we turn back to You.

40 prayers for Your glory to fill our churches and homes mightily, so all the world will see and know that You, alone, are God.

I WAITED PATIENTLY FOR THE LORD; HE TURNED TO ME AND HEARD MY CRY.

— PSALM 40:1 (NIV)

We have cried out to You, Lord, Our Deliverer. Thank you for hearing our cry! Amen!

Your Prayer: Date:

Prayer answered:

DAY 40: THE COMING KING

Then I saw heaven opened, and there was a white horse. Its rider is called Faithful and True, and He judges and makes war in righteousness.

— REVELATION 19:11 (HCSB)

*L*ook up!

Such a strange thing to do in this perilous time. To look up from the shouting, the rioting, the headlines of wars and threats.

To look up from the calamities and the endless political battles and everything that seems important in the here and now.

A King is preparing His return.

His eyes blaze like fire, and His robe is dipped in blood. He will come to bring justice. To judge the nations and wage war.

His name is the Word of God, and in His mouth, he carries a sharp sword. His identity is written on his robe and thigh:

KING OF KINGS AND LORD OF LORDS

Watch! The kings of the earth and generals will gather for the battle, while birds gather for their carrion feast. The armies of Heaven will follow on white horses, gleaming in fine white linen. Then the wrath of the Almighty will be completed and the martyrs will reign with the King.

Oh, Father, I long to see Your Holy City—*the new Jerusalem*—descending from heaven in radiance! *The City where You will dwell with us.*

IN THAT HOLY CITY, THE TEARS I HAVE SHED IN THIS PERILOUS WORLD WILL BE BUT A MEMORY. I'LL NEVER SAY, "GOODBYE!" AGAIN!

Lord, I hold fast to these promises even as the sky darkens above. Even in perilous times!

When wars rage and all is but lost, *I will look up*. I'll lean into the storm to listen for the sound of trumpets *calling me home where I belong:*

LISTEN! *I AM TELLING YOU A MYSTERY:*

WE WILL NOT ALL FALL ASLEEP, BUT WE WILL ALL BE CHANGED, IN A MOMENT, IN THE BLINK OF AN EYE, AT THE LAST TRUMPET.

FOR THE TRUMPET WILL SOUND, AND THE DEAD WILL BE RAISED INCORRUPTIBLE, AND WE WILL BE CHANGED.

— 1 CORINTHIANS 15:51-52 (HCSB)

Look up! The King is coming!

THEN I HEARD SOMETHING LIKE THE VOICE OF A VAST MULTITUDE, LIKE

THE SOUND OF CASCADING WATERS, AND LIKE THE RUMBLING OF LOUD THUNDER, SAYING:

HALLELUJAH, BECAUSE OUR LORD GOD, THE ALMIGHTY, HAS BEGUN TO REIGN!

LET US BE GLAD, REJOICE, AND GIVE HIM GLORY, BECAUSE THE MARRIAGE OF THE LAMB HAS COME, AND HIS WIFE HAS PREPARED HERSELF.

— REVELATION 19:6-7 (HCSB)

Lord, thank you for what is yet to come! Thank you for the endless Hope, the unconditional Love, the all-covering Grace and Your blessed Mercy!

We have all that we need in You!

Why should we be discouraged, Jesus, when Your name is so great? Let's rejoice and praise You for the victory is already won!

Yes, there is an end to these perilous times!

In expectation, I pray, Come, Lord Jesus, come! Amen!

Your Prayer: Date:

_____
_____
_____
_____
_____
_____
_____
_____
_____
_____
_____
_____
_____
_____
_____
_____
_____
_____

Prayer answered:

_____
_____
_____

AFTERWORD

THE KEY TO PRAYING GOD'S PROMISES

Isn't it strange how the enemy attacks when we get close to God's truth? Maybe you, like me, have found that to be true.

The attacks that sting the most are those that come from unexpected places—even from friends, family members, and other believers. Often, the individual doesn't realize that they have precisely pressed a spiritual bruise in our soul.

Thanks to Scripture, however, we can learn to recognize the more familiar methods that our enemy uses to lead us astray. One of which is to try to get us to doubt God's Word and His goodness.

Unfortunately, the enemy can know our weaknesses, too. Whenever someone's words hit just the right sore spot, I know that the enemy behind the attack, and that he is up to no good.

Let me give you an example: While writing these prayers, I participated in an online discussion. In the course of the exchange, I referenced a well-known promise from 2 Chronicles 7:

When I shut up the heavens so that there is no rain, or command locusts

*to devour the land or send a plague among my people, if my people, who
are called by my name, will humble themselves and pray and seek my
face and turn from their wicked ways, then I will hear from heaven, and
I will forgive their sin and will heal their land.*

— 2 CHRONICLES 7:13-14 HCSB

After posting the verse, a woman confronted me. She challenged me, stating that this promise was given by God to the Israelites. For that reason, she commented, God had *no intention of honoring the promise* in the lives of Christian believers such as myself.

Ouch! That confrontation set off a stream of questions in my mind: *Was this true?* Are some promises off-limits to Christians, especially the 2 Chronicles 7 promise that provides specific steps for seeking a healing of the land? Wasn't that what I most wanted? A healing for our nation?

I needed to know the truth.

Whenever the enemy approached Jesus, He withstood the attack by knowing and responding to the enemy with Scripture. We, too, should follow His example, taking any doubt or question directly to God in prayer, and by seeking His Word for answers.

ALL OF THE PROMISES ARE "YES" IN CHRIST

The exciting news is that Scripture confirms that Christians can, in fact, hold on to *each and every promise* found in the Bible. We, like the Israelites, can trust God to honor these wonderful gifts in our lives, too!

In fact, there are *multiple* verses confirming this truth, two of which are these:

*FOR EVERY ONE OF GOD'S PROMISES IS "YES" IN HIM. THEREFORE, THE
"AMEN" IS ALSO SPOKEN THROUGH HIM BY US FOR GOD'S GLORY.*

— 2 CORINTHIANS 1:20 (HCSB)

IF YOU BELONG TO CHRIST, THEN YOU ARE ABRAHAM'S SEED, HEIRS ACCORDING TO THE PROMISE.

— GALATIONS 3:29 (HCSB)

By going to Scripture with my questions, I found answers that *increased my faith*—rather than lessening it as the enemy had ultimately hoped.

Yes, Christians can count on God to honor the promises in His Word, and confidently remind our Father of these treasures in our prayer life.

However, there is one requirement. In order to take hold of these precious promises as our own, we must first be one of the body of Christ. That means we need to have *accepted Jesus as the Savior and Lord of our life.* This is what it means by "belonging to Christ."

THE WAY, THE TRUTH AND THE LIFE

It all comes down to His Love for us, a gift of freewill, and a choice only we can make. God's chose to send His Son, Jesus, to ransom us completely from the penalty of sin—which is eternal separation from God. To be grafted into the wonderful inheritance of promises given by God in the Bible, we must choose to accept Jesus Christ as the Son of Almighty God, believe in His sacrifice, and accept Him as Lord of our life.

It is our choice to make:

FOR GOD SO [GREATLY] LOVED AND DEARLY PRIZED THE WORLD, THAT HE [EVEN] GAVE HIS [ONE AND] [A]ONLY BEGOTTEN SON, SO THAT

WHOEVER BELIEVES AND TRUSTS IN HIM [AS SAVIOR] SHALL NOT PERISH, BUT HAVE ETERNAL LIFE.

— JOHN 3:16 (AMP)

Sometimes, we make it harder than it has to be, but the gospel message is quite simple:

Believe that Jesus is the Son of God, sent by God to be a sacrifice, or a ransom, to pay the full price of our sin, which is eternal death and separation from God. **Trust, then, in this same Jesus as our Lord and Savior,** knowing that as He rose from the dead, we who believe in Him will follow and live eternally with Him.

There is no other requirement other than what the Bible tells us in John 3:16. That decision is the most important decision one can make.

THE PROMISES ARE FOR THE CHILDREN OF GOD

If you believe and receive Jesus as your savior, then you are one of the body of Christ, and are now a "Child of God," as John writes:

HE CAME TO THAT WHICH WAS HIS OWN, BUT HIS OWN DID NOT RECEIVE HIM. YET TO ALL WHO DID RECEIVE HIM, TO THOSE WHO BELIEVED IN HIS NAME, HE GAVE THE RIGHT TO BECOME CHILDREN OF GOD— CHILDREN BORN NOT OF NATURAL DESCENT, NOR OF HUMAN DECISION OR A HUSBAND'S WILL, BUT BORN OF GOD.

— JOHN 1:11-13 (NIV)

As a child of God, you have access to the rich inheritance of promises in God's Word!

CHILD OF GOD, INCLUDE THESE PROMISES IN YOUR PRAYERS WITH CONFIDENCE, KNOWING THAT GOD HEARS YOU AND WILL BE FAITHFUL TO EACH AND EVERY ONE! ISN'T THAT AN EXCITING WAY TO PRAY?

ABOUT THE AUTHOR

Kelly Langston is passionate helping others find the Promised Land that God has prepared for His children. Using Scripture as a road map and God's Promises as fuel for the journey, Kelly believes that every believer can find the extraordinary life that Christ died to give us.

Married to Matt and mother of two vivacious children, Kelly has written professionally since her early days in the journalism school of The Ohio State University writing for *The Lantern*. Her original blog resonated with parents of autistic children from around the world.

Kelly is also the author of *Autism's Hidden Blessings: Discovering God's Promises for Autistic Children and Their Families* published by Kregel Publications.

To learn more, please visit www.kellylangston.com.

Connect with Kelly online:
www.kellylangston.com
info@kellylangston.com

A SPECIAL WORD FROM THE AUTHOR

Thank you for participating in the 40 Prayers for Perilous Times journey. I wrote these prayers in a perilous time, and God has moved in amazing ways.

Now it's your turn:

Would you consider sharing what you have learned in this journey, including how God has responded to your prayers? By sharing, you are lifting up Jesus to a world in desperate need of His Light.

Here is where to share your story:

http://kellylangston.com/40-prayers-for-perilous-times/

Finally, would you consider posting an honest, short review on Amazon? Reviews are the way to help me draw attention to this book and get it into the hands of others who will join the secret army and pray with us. It only takes a few minutes of your time and it makes a difference. *Thank you!*

Finally, keep praying because He is listening! Many blessings to you!

To God be the Kingdom and the Power and the Glory forever... Amen!